A Master Mariner Mindset Smooth Sailing

A Simple Guide to effective Management and Creates Positive Waves

By: Mustafa Nejem

CONTENTS

Chapter 1

Introduction to Effective Management
Introduce the concept of "Smooth Sailing" in management.

Within the endless ocean of administration, embracing the Captain Sailor Mentality can change your authority fashion into a signal of successful administration. At the heart of this mentality lies the concept of "Smooth Cruising." Fair as a talented captain navigates turbulent waters to guarantee a calm voyage, a fruitful director can make an environment that cultivates efficiency and positivity. Let's explore how you'll be able present the concept of "Smooth Cruising" in your administration approach.

Understanding Smooth Sailing:
- Imagine your team as a ship, and you, the manager, as the captain. Smooth Sailing is the art of navigating challenges and uncertainties with finesse, ensuring that your team reaches its destination with minimal turbulence.
- Emphasize the importance of foreseeing potential obstacles, addressing conflicts, and steering the team towards success.
- Just as a captain studies weather patterns, a manager must analyze the organizational landscape to ensure a smooth journey.

Communication as Your Nautical Chart:
- In navigation, charts guide a ship through the sea. Similarly, effective communication acts as the nautical chart for your team, ensuring everyone is on the same course.
- Encourage open and transparent communication within your team. Clearly articulate goals, expectations, and the overall vision. Just as a captain updates the crew on the route, keep your team informed about the organization's mission and the path to achieve it.

Adapting to Changing Tides:
- Seas are dynamic, and so is the business environment. A flexible approach is vital for navigating through unexpected challenges, just as a captain adjusts sails to changing winds.
- Foster a culture of adaptability within your team. Encourage them to embrace change and be proactive in finding innovative solutions. Show by example that adapting to new circumstances is a strength, not a weakness.

Creating a Collaborative Seascape:
- Picture your team as diverse islands in an archipelago, interconnected by the same sea. Just as islands depend on each other for sustenance, fostering collaboration among team members creates a synergy that propels the entire team forward.
- Encourage teamwork by assigning projects that require collective efforts. Establish platforms for open discussions, where every crew member has the opportunity to contribute ideas. Emphasize that success is a shared journey, and the strength of the team lies in its unity.

The Symphony of Recognition:
- Much like the captain acknowledging a job well done by the crew, recognizing and celebrating achievements creates a harmonious atmosphere that resonates throughout the team.
- Implement a system of regular recognition for individual and team accomplishments. This can be as simple as public acknowledgments during team meetings or more formalized recognition programs. Celebrate milestones, both big and small, as they contribute to the overall success of the journey.

Weathering Storms Together:
- Storms at sea test the resilience of a crew. Similarly, in the professional landscape, challenges are inevitable. Fostering a sense of camaraderie prepares the team to weather storms together.
- During challenging times, act as the captain who rallies the crew. Encourage open communication about the difficulties and collaboratively strategize solutions. Highlight past instances where the team overcame obstacles, reinforcing the collective strength that arises from unity.

Investing in Crew Well-being:
- Just as a captain ensures the crew's well-being by providing a safe and comfortable ship, prioritize the well-being of your team members.
- Implement initiatives that support work-life balance, mental health, and professional development. Actively listen to concerns and provide resources to address challenges. A content and well-supported crew is more likely to contribute positively to the overall sailing experience.

Importance of positive leadership.

Inside the broad oceans of compelling administration, the Captain Sailor Mentality places a solid accentuation on the significance of positive authority. Fair as a talented captain shapes the temperament on a dispatch, a positive pioneer has the control to impact the whole team's flow. Let's reveal the centrality of positive authority and how it adjusts with the reasoning of smooth cruising .

Setting the Tone for Smooth Sailing:
- The captain is the heartbeat of the ship, setting the tone for the entire crew. Similarly, a positive leader influences the team's energy and attitude, paving the way for a smooth managerial journey.
- Demonstrate optimism and enthusiasm in your leadership approach. Your attitude will be mirrored by the team. Just as a captain's calm demeanor soothes the crew, your positivity will alleviate stress and create a conducive work environment.

Building Trust in Your Leadership Lighthouse:
- A lighthouse guides ships safely to shore.
- A positive leader acts as a beacon of trust, guiding the team through challenges and uncertainties.
- Foster trust through consistent and transparent communication. Just as a captain's decisions instill confidence in the crew, your team should trust your judgment. Be open, honest, and reliable, and your leadership will serve as a guiding light during challenging times.

Cultivating Resilience in Stormy Weather:
- Storms are inevitable at sea, but a resilient crew weathers them successfully. Similarly, positive leadership instills resilience in the team, enabling them to overcome obstacles.
- Encourage a growth mindset within your team. Emphasize learning from challenges and view them as opportunities for improvement. Just as a captain's resilience inspires the crew during storms, your positivity in the face of adversity will motivate your team to persevere.

Amplifying Team Collaboration through Positivity:
- A united crew is a powerful force against rough seas. Positive leadership strengthens team bonds, fostering collaboration and synergy.
- Encourage teamwork and collaboration. Celebrate individual and collective achievements. Just as a captain unites the crew for a common goal, your positive leadership will bring your team together, enhancing their collective effectiveness.

Preview of the book's approach and journey

Setting out on the Captain Sailor Attitude travel is associated to setting cruise on a voyage of viable administration. Some time recently we jump into the complexities, let's take a minute to see the approach and travel that will direct you through the waves of positive authority and smooth cruising.

Navigating the Captain Mariner Mindset Compass:

- Just as a captain relies on a compass to navigate the sea, your management compass is the Captain Mariner Mindset. It directs you towards effective leadership and smooth sailing.
- We will explore key aspects of this mindset, including understanding the waters of management, fostering positive leadership, and cultivating a harmonious crew spirit. Each point contributes to the overall success of your managerial voyage.

The Chapters of Smooth Sailing:

- Picture each chapter as a stretch of calm seas, with insights and strategies to conquer managerial challenges.
  Each chapter builds upon the last, creating a comprehensive guide for effective leadership.
- We will delve into practical applications, incorporating the Captain Mariner Mindset into your everyday managerial decisions. From communication strategies to adaptability, you'll gain the tools to navigate any professional sea.

Interactive Ports of Reflection:

- Just as a ship stops at ports for reflection, our guide includes moments for you to pause and reflect on your managerial journey. These interactive sections provide an opportunity to internalize key concepts.
- Engage with the guide actively. Consider how each concept applies to your managerial style, fostering a deeper understanding of the Captain Mariner Mindset and its impact on your team.

Your Personalized Map for Success:

- A captain crafts a unique map for their voyage. Similarly, you will develop a personalized map for effective management, incorporating the principles of the Captain Mariner Mindset.
- By the end of this guide, you'll have a customized approach to management that aligns with your leadership style. Your map will guide you through any managerial waters, ensuring a successful and positive journey.

Chapter 2

The Captain's Mindset

Discuss the importance of a leader's mentality

In the tremendous scope of successful administration, the Captain Sailor Mentality places critical accentuation on the leader's attitude as the guiding drive for the whole group. Fair as a captain's mindset shapes the course of a transport, a leader's mentality impacts the course, culture, and victory of a group. Let's dig into the significance of a leader's mindset and how it adjusts with the reasoning of smooth cruising.

The Captain's Mindset as the Helm:
- Envision the captain's mindset as the helm of the ship, determining its direction. Similarly, a leader's mentality is the guiding force steering the team towards success.
- Recognize that your mentality serves as the helm for your team's journey. Whether through calm waters or storms, a positive and focused mindset allows you to navigate challenges and lead the team with clarity and purpose.

Influence on Decision-Making:
- A captain's mentality shapes critical decisions at sea.
  Similarly, a leader's mindset influences decision-making processes within the organization.
- Be aware that your mentality directly impacts the choices you make. A positive and strategic mindset contributes to well-informed decisions. By aligning your thinking with the organization's goals, you guide the team towards success.

Cultivating a Culture of Resilience:
- A captain's resilient mentality is crucial during storms. Similarly, a leader's resilient mindset fosters a culture of perseverance and adaptability.
- Demonstrate resilience in the face of challenges. Encourage your team to view setbacks as opportunities for growth. Just as a captain's determined mindset boosts the crew's morale during turbulent times, your resilient mentality inspires the team to overcome obstacles.

Building Trust Through Consistency:
- A captain's consistent mentality builds trust among the crew. Similarly, a leader's consistent mindset creates a foundation of trust within the team.
- Strive for consistency in your approach.
  Whether in communication, decision-making, or problem-solving, a reliable and steady mentality fosters trust. This trust becomes the anchor that stabilizes the team even in uncertain waters.

Captain's Innovative Thinking:
- Picture a captain contemplating uncharted territories, devising innovative routes for the ship's success. Similarly, a leader's creative mentality is the compass guiding the team through unexplored challenges.
- Recognize the importance of innovative thinking. Encourage your team to approach problems with a fresh perspective. Much like a captain who charts new courses for efficiency, your forward-thinking mentality will inspire the team to explore inventive solutions and discover new avenues for growth.

Embracing a Creative Mindset:

- A captain's ability to think creatively ensures the ship's adaptability in unpredictable seas. Similarly, a leader's creative mindset fosters adaptability and resilience within the team.
- Cultivate a culture that embraces creativity. Provide space for brainstorming, idea-sharing, and experimentation.

  Just as a captain adapts to changing conditions, your creative mindset encourages the team to explore different approaches, sparking innovation and promoting a dynamic work environment.

Motivating Exploration of Inventive Solutions:

- A captain explores various routes for the ship's success. Likewise, a leader's mentality motivates the team to explore inventive solutions to challenges.
- Inspire a mindset of curiosity and experimentation. Encourage your team to seek out novel solutions, even if they involve stepping into uncharted territories. As a captain searches for the most efficient path, your leadership mentality motivates the team to contribute innovative ideas, driving progress and success.

Creating an Atmosphere of Continuous Improvement:

- A captain's commitment to improvement ensures the ship's efficiency. Similarly, a leader's creative mentality creates an atmosphere where continuous improvement is valued.
- Communicate the importance of continuous learning and improvement. Just as a captain seeks ways to enhance the ship's performance, your creative leadership mentality encourages the team to.

Aligning personal values with leadership goals.

Within the endless sea of compelling administration, the Captain Sailor Mentality welcomes pioneers to set cruise with a significant understanding of adjusting individual values with administration objectives. Fair as a captain adjusts the ship's course with navigational charts, a fruitful pioneer must explore their administrative travel by harmonizing individual values with organizational goals. Let's investigate the significance of this arrangement and how it contributes to the logic of smooth cruising.

Personal Values as the North Star:

- Just as a captain relies on the North Star for direction, leaders should anchor their decisions in their core values. Personal values act as a guiding light in the managerial journey.
- Reflect on your personal values and how they align with your leadership goals. Ensure that your actions and decisions resonate with your ethical compass. By doing so, you set a consistent and reliable course for your team, creating stability and trust.

Navigating Choppy Waters of Ethical Dilemmas:

- The sea of business often presents ethical challenges.

  A captain's adherence to principles during storms is akin to a leader navigating through ethical dilemmas while upholding personal values.
- Communicate the importance of ethical decision-making to your team. Showcase how your values guide you through challenging situations. Just as a captain maintains integrity in turbulent seas, your commitment to ethical leadership becomes a beacon for your team.

Inspiring a Crew Aligned with Core Values:

- A crew that shares common values is more cohesive. Similarly, a leader should inspire a team that resonates with the organization's values.
- Communicate the organization's core values and foster a team culture that aligns with them. Ensure that hiring, training, and development efforts prioritize individuals who share these values. Just as a captain builds a crew with shared values, you'll cultivate a harmonious and motivated team.

The Captain's Steady Hand:
- Consider the captain as the steady hand on the ship's wheel, maintaining a consistent direction. Similarly, leaders should be unwavering in their commitment to guiding the team in alignment with organizational values.
- Cultivate a mindset of steadfastness in your decision-making. Evaluate each choice against the broader context of the organization's mission and values. This reliability becomes the compass that guides the team through uncertain waters.

Striving for Ethical Excellence:
- A captain's adherence to ethical principles is mirrored in a leader's commitment to ethical excellence. Just as a captain avoids treacherous waters, leaders should steer clear of compromising their ethical standards.
- When faced with ethical dilemmas, prioritize choices that uphold both your personal values and the ethical standards of the organization. This commitment to integrity not only strengthens your moral compass but also sets a powerful example for your team.

Aligning Decisions with Organizational Goals:
- A captain adjusts the ship's course to align with the intended destination. Likewise, leaders must adjust their decisions to align with the overarching goals of the organization.
- Regularly reassess your decisions against the strategic objectives of the organization. Ensure that your choices contribute positively to the achievement of these goals.

The effect of mindset on the team

In the expansive seas of effective management, the Captain Mariner Mindset places a spotlight on the profound impact that a leader's mindset can have on the team. Much like the wind influencing the direction of a ship, a manager's mindset shapes the course and culture of the team. Let's explore how understanding and embodying the Captain Mariner Mindset can create positive waves through the effect of mindset on the team.

The Captain as the Wind:
- Imagine the captain's mindset as the wind that fills the sails, propelling the ship forward. Similarly, a manager's mindset influences the team's direction, energy, and overall work atmosphere.
- Recognize the power of your mindset in shaping team dynamics. Just as a captain adjusts the sails to harness the wind's energy, consciously align your mindset with positivity, resilience, and a solution-oriented approach. This adjustment becomes the driving force that pushes the team towards success.

Setting the Team's Emotional Climate:
- The captain's demeanor affects the emotional climate on the ship. Likewise, a manager's mindset sets the tone for the team's emotional well-being.
- Be aware of your emotional presence as a leader. A positive and optimistic mindset creates an uplifting atmosphere, fostering motivation and enthusiasm. Conversely, a negative mindset can create stormy emotional weather. Strive to be the calm and steady force that assures the team during challenging times.

Influence on Team Morale and Productivity:
- A captain's optimistic outlook boosts the crew's morale, enhancing productivity. Similarly, a positive manager's mindset creates a ripple effect, influencing the team's overall performance.
- Cultivate an optimistic mindset and share it with your team. Celebrate achievements, no matter how small, and acknowledge hard work. Just as a captain motivates the crew through encouragement, your positive mindset becomes a catalyst for increased morale and productivity.

Fostering a Growth Mindset Culture:

A captain's belief in the crew's potential mirrors a leader's commitment to fostering a growth mindset. Embrace challenges as opportunities for improvement.

- Encourage a culture of continuous learning and development. Just as a captain invests in the crew's skills, invest in your team's growth. Promote a mindset that views setbacks as learning experiences, inspiring innovation and resilience.

Creating a Cohesive Team Experience:

- A captain's mindset of unity contributes to a cohesive team. Similarly, a leader's mindset shapes the team experience.
- Strive for a mindset that values collaboration and teamwork. Communicate the importance of unity and create an inclusive environment. Just as a captain fosters camaraderie among the crew, your mindset contributes to a cohesive and harmonious team experience.

Chapter 3

Assembling Your Crew
Effective hiring practices.

Just as a captain meticulously selects a skilled and diverse crew for a smooth sailing experience, effective hiring practices play a pivotal role in the Captain Mariner Mindset of effective management. This guide explores how the principles of navigating the seas can be applied to creating a team that not only weather challenges but thrives in the ever-changing organizational landscape.

Selecting Crew Members for Skill and Fit:
- A captain carefully chooses crew members based on their skills and compatibility with the ship's mission. Similarly, effective hiring practices involve selecting individuals with the right skills and cultural fit for the organization.
- Prioritize a thorough assessment of candidates' skills and alignment with the organizational culture. Just as a captain ensures each crew member contributes to the ship's success, your hiring practices should focus on building a team where each member complements the overall goals and values of the organization.

Navigating the Talent Seas:
- A captain scouts for talented individuals who bring diverse skills to the crew. Likewise, effective hiring involves scouting for talent that adds depth and versatility to the team.
- Actively seek out diverse talent that contributes unique skills and perspectives. Just as a captain values a diverse crew to handle various aspects of the journey, your hiring practices should aim to build a well-rounded team capable of navigating the challenges of the dynamic business environment.

Conducting Thorough Background Checks:
- A captain verifies the backgrounds and experiences of potential crew members. Similarly, effective hiring practices include thorough background checks to ensure the reliability and integrity of potential team members.
- Implement robust background checks to verify candidates' credentials and work history. Just as a captain needs trustworthy crew members, your hiring process should aim to bring individuals on board who align with the organization's values and contribute to a positive and trustworthy team dynamic.

Promoting a Collaborative Onboarding Process:
- A captain ensures a smooth onboarding process for new crew members. Effective hiring practices involve creating a collaborative onboarding process that integrates new team members seamlessly.
- Develop an onboarding process that promotes collaboration and integration. Facilitate interactions between new hires and existing team members, fostering a sense of camaraderie. Just as a captain eases new crew members into their roles, your onboarding practices should help new employees feel welcome and prepared for their responsibilities.

Captain's Adaptive Leadership Styles:
- Imagine a captain steering a ship through diverse waters, adapting leadership styles to different crew dynamics. Similarly, a leader's hiring practices should consider the adaptability needed for the evolving challenges within a team.
- Acknowledge the diversity within your team and understand that each member may require a unique leadership approach. In hiring, prioritize candidates who exhibit versatility and can adapt their skills and communication styles to fit the team's dynamics.

Selecting for Adaptability and Flexibility:
- A captain values crew members who can adapt to changing conditions at sea. Similarly, effective hiring practices involve selecting individuals who demonstrate adaptability and flexibility.
- Look for candidates who have a track record of successfully navigating change. In interviews, inquire about their experiences in dynamic environments and how they've adjusted to evolving circumstances. Just as a captain values a crew that can handle shifting winds, your hiring practices should identify individuals capable of thriving in a changing organizational landscape.

Navigating Shifting Organizational Landscapes:
- A captain anticipates and navigates through changing weather conditions. Likewise, effective hiring practices involve identifying candidates who can navigate and contribute positively to the team's success in shifting organizational landscapes.
- Assess a candidate's ability to handle ambiguity and uncertainty. Pose scenarios that require adaptability and observe how they approach problem-solving. By hiring individuals who can navigate smoothly through changing conditions, you ensure the team remains resilient and effective.

Building a diverse and dynamic team.
Fair as a captain collects a assorted and energetic group to explore the complexities of the ocean, successful administration includes building a group that mirrors these qualities. The Captain Sailor Mentality emphasizes the significance of differing qualities and dynamism for a smooth and fruitful voyage. Let's investigate how the standards of collecting a safe group can be connected to building a assorted and energetic group within the domain of successful administration.

Crew Diversity Mirrors Team Strength:
- A captain selects crew members with diverse skills, strengths, and backgrounds to enhance the ship's capabilities. Similarly, effective management involves building a diverse team to leverage a broad range of skills and perspectives.
- Embrace diversity in hiring by considering candidates from various backgrounds, experiences, and skill sets. Just as a captain values a crew with a mix of talents to handle different ship tasks, your team will thrive with a diverse blend of skills and perspectives.

Navigating Complex Waters with Varied Expertise:
- A captain values crew members with different expertise for handling diverse challenges at sea. Likewise, building a dynamic team involves bringing together individuals with varied skills to navigate complex organizational waters.
- Identify the specific skills and expertise needed within your team and seek individuals who bring diverse strengths. This diversity equips the team to navigate a variety of challenges successfully. Just as a captain values crew members with different expertise for handling diverse challenges at sea, your team will thrive with a diverse blend of skills and perspectives.

Strengthening Team Resilience Through Variety:
- A captain knows that a diverse crew enhances the ship's resilience in the face of adversity. Similarly, a diverse team in management strengthens resilience by offering various approaches to problem-solving.
- Build a team that can adapt to changing circumstances by incorporating individuals with different perspectives. Just as a captain values a resilient crew, your diverse team will be better equipped to handle unforeseen challenges and find innovative solutions.

Creating an Inclusive Team Culture:
- A captain fosters inclusivity to create a cohesive crew. In effective management, building a diverse team requires creating an inclusive culture where every member feels valued and heard.

- Prioritize inclusivity in team culture. Encourage open communication and collaboration, ensuring that each team member's voice is heard. Just as a captain values an inclusive crew for optimal teamwork, your team's diversity will flourish in an environment that promotes mutual respect and understanding.

Harvesting Innovation from Diversity:
- A captain recognizes that diverse perspectives foster innovation at sea. Similarly, a diverse team in management cultivates innovation by bringing together varied viewpoints and approaches.
- Encourage creativity and innovation by valuing diverse perspectives. Just as a captain values the innovation that arises from diverse crew members, your team will generate fresh ideas and creative solutions through the richness of its diversity.

The role of team chemistry

Effective management, much like sailing, thrives on the synergy and harmony of a well-knit crew. The Captain Mariner Mindset emphasizes the importance of team chemistry—a vital force that propels the ship of success through the waters of challenges and triumphs. Let's explore the analogy of team chemistry and its pivotal role in the overall effectiveness of a team.

Captain as the Maestro of Harmony:
- Picture the captain as a maestro orchestrating harmony among the diverse instruments of a crew. Similarly, a leader's role is to conduct and cultivate team chemistry.
- Recognize that each team member contributes a unique skill, much like instruments in an orchestra. Encourage collaboration, open communication, and mutual respect. Just as a captain ensures that every crew member plays their part, you, as a leader, create an environment where individual strengths harmonize to create a powerful team symphony.

Creating a Unified Crew Symphony:
- A captain strives for a unified crew working in synchrony. Likewise, effective management requires creating a team that operates as a cohesive and synchronized unit.
- Emphasize the importance of shared goals and a collective mission. Fostering a sense of belonging and purpose among team members enhances team chemistry. Just as a captain ensures the crew follows a common course, you guide your team to work collaboratively towards shared objectives, ensuring smooth sailing through the challenges that lie ahead.

Navigating Through Diversity:
- A captain navigates through diverse seas, and similarly, a leader must navigate through diverse talents and personalities within the team.
- Recognize the strength in diversity. Each team member brings a unique set of skills and perspectives. Acknowledge and celebrate these differences, fostering an inclusive environment. Just as a captain values the diverse skills of the crew, you, as a leader, harness the power of diverse talents to navigate through the complexities of the professional landscape.

Cultivating Open Communication Channels:
- On a ship, effective communication is crucial for smooth sailing. Similarly, in a team, open communication is the wind that fills the sails of productivity.
- Promote an open and transparent communication culture. Encourage team members to share ideas, provide feedback, and express concerns freely. Just as a captain relies on effective communication to guide the ship, you rely on clear communication channels to steer your team toward success.

Building Trust as the Anchor of Chemistry:
- A captain's trust in the crew is the anchor that holds the ship steady. Likewise, trust is the foundation of team chemistry in effective management.
- Establish and nurture trust among team members. Trust fosters a sense of security and collaboration. Just as a captain trusts the crew to perform their roles, you build trust by empowering and relying on your team, creating a strong anchor that keeps the team grounded even in turbulent times.

Chapter 4

Navigation Basics
Setting clear goals and expectations

In the Captain Mariner Mindset, setting clear goals and expectations is akin to charting a precise course for a ship. As a leader, your role is to act as the navigator, providing a clear direction for your team amidst the vast sea of tasks and challenges. Let's delve into the analogy of setting clear goals and expectations and understand how it contributes to effective management and positive waves.

Captain as the Navigator:
- Envision the captain as the navigator of the ship, plotting a course through uncharted waters. Similarly, a leader must navigate the organizational landscape by setting a clear direction through well-defined goals and expectations.
- Assume the role of the captain by charting a clear course for your team. Clearly define the goals, both short-term and long-term, and communicate the expectations for achieving them.
- Just as a captain ensures the ship follows a precise route, your leadership ensures the team is aligned with the strategic direction of the organization.

Mapping the Course of Success:
- A captain meticulously maps the course to reach the intended destination. Likewise, as a leader, you must map out the path to success through well-defined goals.
- Establish a roadmap that outlines the steps required to achieve the goals. Break down larger objectives into manageable tasks, creating a clear and achievable route. Just as a captain maps out a safe passage, your strategic planning ensures the team navigates towards success without unnecessary detours.

Clarity as the North Star:
- The North Star guides a ship through the night. Similarly, clarity in goals and expectations acts as the North Star for the team, providing direction in challenging times.
- Ensure absolute clarity in your communication regarding goals and expectations. Make them visible and easily accessible to the entire team.
  Just as a captain relies on the North Star for navigation, your team should be able to rely on the clarity of goals to steer their efforts in the right direction.

Aligning Team Efforts:
- A captain aligns the ship's crew to work towards a common goal. Likewise, as a leader, your role is to align your team's efforts towards the achievement of shared objectives.
- Communicate the bigger picture to your team, emphasizing how individual efforts contribute to the overall success. Just as a captain ensures everyone works in harmony, your leadership aligns the team's efforts, fostering collaboration and a sense of collective purpose.

Captain's Course Adjustments:
- Imagine a captain navigating through varying weather conditions, adjusting the ship's course for optimal safety and efficiency. Similarly, leaders must be ready to adapt goals and expectations to suit the ever-changing dynamics of the organization.
- Stay vigilant to changes in the external environment, such as market trends, technological advancements, or shifts in customer preferences.
  Regularly reassess organizational goals in light of these changes. Just as a captain navigates changing conditions at sea, your leadership ensures the team remains responsive to the evolving external factors affecting the organization.

Vigilance and Flexibility:
- A captain stays vigilant for potential storms and navigational challenges. Similarly, effective leaders must be vigilant to changes in the business landscape and be willing to adjust goals accordingly.
- Keep a watchful eye on industry trends, competitor activities, and any other external factors that may impact your organization. Encourage flexibility within the team to adapt to unforeseen circumstances.

Dynamic Goal Setting:
- A captain dynamically sets the ship's course based on current conditions. Likewise, leaders should dynamically set goals that align with the organization's evolving needs.
- Establish a goal-setting process that allows for regular reviews and adjustments. Goals should be aligned with the organization's vision, but also adaptable to changing circumstances.

Aligning individual roles with the company vision

Just as a captain ensures that each crew member's role contributes to the overall journey's success, effective leaders with the Captain Mariner Mindset align individual roles with the company vision. This analogy emphasizes the importance of harmonizing individual efforts to propel the entire organization towards its overarching goals. Let's explore the application of this mindset in effective management.

Captain's Crew Roles:
- Picture a captain assigning specific roles to each crew member based on their strengths and expertise. Similarly, leaders align individual roles within the team with the company's vision and objectives.
- Assess the unique skills and strengths of each team member. Assign responsibilities that align with both individual capabilities and the broader organizational vision. Just as a captain ensures each crew member plays a vital role, your leadership ensures that every team member contributes meaningfully to the company's overarching goals.

Ensuring Role Relevance to the Vision:
- A captain ensures that every crew member's task is relevant to the ship's journey. Likewise, leaders ensure that individual roles directly contribute to the company's vision and mission.
- Regularly revisit and realign individual roles with the company's vision. Confirm that tasks and responsibilities remain relevant to organizational objectives. Just as a captain constantly adjusts crew tasks for optimal efficiency, your leadership ensures that each team member's contribution aligns with the evolving needs of the company.

Communicating the Big Picture:
- A captain communicates the ship's destination to the crew. Similarly, leaders should effectively communicate the company's vision, ensuring that each team member understands their role in achieving it.
- Clearly articulate the company's vision and how each individual's role contributes to the larger picture. Foster a sense of purpose and connection to the organizational mission.
  Just as a captain ensures the crew understands the journey's purpose, your leadership aligns individual roles by emphasizing their significance in achieving the company's overarching vision.

Empowering Individuals as Contributors:
- A captain empowers crew members to contribute to the ship's success. Likewise, leaders empower individuals by acknowledging their role as valuable contributors to the company's vision.
- Encourage autonomy and decision-making within individual roles. Recognize and celebrate achievements that directly impact the realization of the company's vision.

Just as a captain empowers the crew for success, your leadership style empowers individuals to make meaningful contributions aligned with the company's strategic objectives.

Decision-making strategies

The Captain Mariner Mindset recognizes that effective decision-making is the compass that guides a leader through the unpredictable seas of management. Drawing an analogy from a captain navigating a ship, this guide explores decision-making strategies that ensure smooth sailing and create positive waves in the realm of effective management.

Captain's Charted Course:
- Just as a captain charts a course based on charts, maps, and navigational expertise, leaders must have a well-defined decision-making framework.
- Develop a systematic approach to decision-making. Utilize data, insights, and strategic thinking to chart the course for the organization. Establish clear criteria and guidelines for decision-making, ensuring a well-informed and purposeful direction.

Navigating by Organizational Values:
- A captain's decisions are guided by the ship's values and safety protocols. Similarly, leaders should align decisions with the organization's core values and principles.
- Prioritize decisions that align with the company's values. Evaluate options based on their adherence to ethical standards and long-term organizational goals. Just as a captain ensures decisions are in line with maritime principles, your leadership aligns choices with the organization's values.

Consideration of External Factors:
- A captain considers weather conditions and external factors when navigating. Likewise, leaders should factor in external elements like market trends and competitor activities in decision-making.
- Stay informed about external factors that may impact the organization. Conduct thorough analyses and risk assessments before making decisions. Much like a captain adapts to changing weather conditions, your leadership adjusts strategies based on the dynamic external landscape.

Crew Consultation and Collaboration:
- A captain may consult with the crew for insights. Similarly, leaders should foster a culture of collaboration, seeking input from team members in decision-making.
- Encourage open communication and collaboration within the team. Seek diverse perspectives to enrich the decision-making process. Just as a captain values the insights of the crew, your leadership values the collective wisdom of the team to make well-rounded decisions.

Course Corrections and Adaptability:
- A captain adjusts the ship's course as needed. Effective leaders embrace adaptability and are open to course corrections in response to evolving circumstances.
- Be willing to reassess and adapt decisions when necessary. Monitor outcomes, seek feedback, and adjust strategies as the situation evolves. Like a captain adjusting the ship's course to reach the destination, your leadership ensures flexibility to achieve the organization's goals in dynamic environments.

Chapter **5**

Plotting the Course
Strategic planning for short-term and long-term success.

Much like a captain charting a course for a voyage, effective management requires strategic planning that encompasses both short-term maneuvers and long-term aspirations. The Captain Mariner Mindset encourages leaders to navigate the organizational waters with a comprehensive strategy that ensures not only smooth sailing in the present but also a steady course towards long-term success.

Captain's Voyage Itinerary:
- A captain plans the ship's itinerary for the entire journey. Similarly, leaders must develop a comprehensive strategic plan that outlines both short-term objectives and long-term goals.
- Create a roadmap that outlines the organization's journey, including short-term milestones and long-term objectives. Ensure that every strategic decision aligns with this itinerary. Just as a captain plans the route, your leadership strategically maps out the organization's course for sustained success.

Short-Term Maneuvers in Response to Immediate Conditions:
- A captain may alter the ship's course for short-term maneuvers in response to immediate conditions. Similarly, leaders should have strategies in place for short-term adjustments based on current organizational conditions.
- Develop contingency plans and agile strategies to respond to immediate challenges. These short-term maneuvers should align with the overall strategic plan. Like a captain adapting to sudden weather changes, your leadership ensures the organization remains nimble in response to unforeseen circumstances.

Setting Sail for Long-Term Horizons:
- A captain sets sail with the long-term destination in mind. Leaders should establish clear long-term goals that guide the organization's overall direction.
- Define ambitious yet achievable long-term objectives. These goals serve as the North Star for decision-making and resource allocation. Just as a captain aims for a distant port, your leadership guides the organization towards sustainable success in the long run.

Continuous Monitoring of the Navigational Compass:
- A captain constantly monitors the ship's navigational instruments. Similarly, leaders should regularly assess and adjust their strategies, ensuring they stay on course for both short-term and long-term success.
- Implement a system for monitoring key performance indicators and adjusting strategies based on performance reviews. Regularly reassess the strategic plan to adapt to changing internal and external conditions. Like a captain staying vigilant, your leadership ensures the organization remains on track and resilient.

Collaborative Navigation with the Crew:
- A captain collaborates with the crew to navigate. Similarly, leaders should involve the entire team in the strategic planning process, fostering a sense of collective ownership.
- Encourage open communication and collaboration in the strategic planning process. Seek insights from various team members to ensure a well-rounded perspective. Just as a captain relies on the expertise of the crew, your leadership benefits from the collective intelligence and commitment of the team to steer the organization towards success.

Adapting Strategies to Changing Tides:
- A captain adjusts the ship's strategy based on changing tides. Leaders should be ready to adapt strategies to changing market trends, technological advancements, and other external factors.
- Stay informed about industry shifts and evolving market conditions. Be prepared to modify strategies to capitalize on emerging opportunities or mitigate potential risks. Like a captain adjusting the ship's strategy to navigate changing tides, your leadership ensures the organization remains responsive and competitive.

Adapting to change and uncertainty.

In the dynamic waters of effective management, the ability to adapt to change and uncertainty is paramount. Much like a captain navigating through unpredictable seas, leaders with the Captain Mariner Mindset understand the importance of flexibility and resilience in steering the ship of their organization. Let's explore the analogies that guide leaders in embracing change and uncertainty for smooth sailing.

Captain's Course Corrections:
- A captain adjusts the ship's course when faced with unexpected currents. Similarly, leaders must be prepared to make course corrections in response to changes and uncertainties.
- Cultivate a mindset that welcomes feedback and embraces the need for adjustments. Regularly reassess strategies and be willing to change direction when necessary. Just as a captain ensures the ship stays on course, your leadership adapts to evolving circumstances, ensuring the organization remains on a path to success.

Navigating Uncharted Waters:
- A captain navigates through uncharted waters, adapting to the unknown. Likewise, leaders navigate through uncertainties, adapting strategies to tackle unfamiliar challenges.
- Foster a culture of curiosity and courage within the organization. Encourage the team to explore new territories, experiment with innovative solutions, and embrace the unknown. Like a captain navigating through uncharted waters, your leadership thrives in uncertainty, turning challenges into opportunities for growth.

Weathering Storms of Change:
- A captain steers the ship through storms, adapting to turbulent conditions. Leaders must guide their teams through organizational storms, adapting to turbulent changes.
- Develop resilience within the team to weather periods of uncertainty. Provide support, communicate transparently, and ensure the team remains united in the face of change. Much like a captain guides the ship through storms, your leadership steers the organization through challenges, ensuring it emerges stronger on the other side.

Embracing an Agile Crew Mentality:
- A captain relies on an agile crew to respond swiftly to changing conditions. Leaders should foster an agile mentality within the organization, enabling quick and effective responses to changes.
- Encourage a culture of adaptability and nimbleness. Equip the team with the tools and mindset to pivot swiftly when needed. Just as a captain's agile crew responds to shifting winds, your leadership ensures the organization is responsive and adaptable in the face of uncertainty.

Strategic Use of Navigation Instruments:
- A captain relies on navigation instruments to navigate. Leaders must utilize data and insights as their navigation instruments, making informed decisions in uncertain conditions.
- Invest in data analytics and gather insights to inform decision-making. Utilize information to navigate through uncertainty and make strategic choices that align with

the organization's goals. Like a captain using navigation instruments to navigate the seas, your leadership relies on data for informed decision-making in the turbulent waters of change.

Importance of flexibility and contingency planning.

In the ever-changing seas of effective management, the importance of flexibility and contingency planning cannot be overstated. Drawing inspiration from the Captain Mariner Mindset, which navigates through unpredictable waters, this guide explores the analogies that illuminate the significance of adaptability and strategic contingency planning for smooth sailing in the realm of effective management.

Sailing with the Winds of Flexibility:

- A captain adjusts sails to harness the changing winds. Similarly, leaders must embrace flexibility to adapt to evolving conditions in the business environment.
- Cultivate a culture where flexibility is valued. Encourage team members to be open to new ideas and approaches. Like a captain adjusting sails for optimal performance, your leadership ensures that the organization harnesses the power of flexibility to navigate challenges effectively.

Navigating Through Unforeseen Waves:

- A captain navigates through unexpected waves, adjusting the ship's course. Leaders should be prepared to navigate unforeseen challenges by adjusting strategies and plans.
- Develop a mindset that anticipates potential disruptions. Establish contingency plans for various scenarios, ensuring the organization is well-prepared to respond to unexpected waves. Much like a captain navigates through unpredictable waves, your leadership navigates through uncertainties with adaptability and resilience.

Weathering the Storms of Change:

- A captain ensures the ship is resilient during storms. Leaders must build organizational resilience to weather the storms of change.
- Create contingency plans that enable the organization to endure periods of turbulence. Implement risk management strategies to mitigate potential negative impacts. Like a captain ensuring the ship is well-prepared for storms, your leadership fortifies the organization against the adversities of change.

Relying on the Anchor of Contingency Planning:

- A captain relies on the anchor for stability. Leaders should anchor their strategies with robust contingency plans to provide stability during uncertainties.
- Develop comprehensive contingency plans that encompass various aspects of the organization, from operations to finances. Ensure the team is aware of these plans, ready to implement them when needed. Similar to a captain relying on the anchor for stability, your leadership establishes contingency planning as the anchor that keeps the organization steady during turbulent times.

Strategic Maneuvers in Response to Challenges:

- A captain employs strategic maneuvers to navigate challenges. Leaders should employ strategic contingency maneuvers to address unexpected challenges.
- Regularly review and update contingency plans based on changing conditions. Implement strategic maneuvers that align with the organization's goals, ensuring a smooth response to challenges. Like a captain using strategic maneuvers, your leadership executes well-thought-out plans to navigate uncertainties effectively.

Chapter **6**

The Art of Delegation
Identifying strengths and assigning tasks.

Much like a captain carefully assigns roles to the crew based on their strengths and expertise, effective leaders with the Captain Mariner Mindset recognize the importance of identifying individual strengths and strategically assigning tasks. This analogical guide explores how aligning team members' strengths with specific responsibilities contributes to smooth sailing in the realm of effective management.

Captain's Crew Expertise Allocation:
- A captain assigns specific tasks to crew members based on their skills and expertise. Similarly, leaders must identify the strengths of their team members and allocate tasks accordingly.
- Conduct thorough assessments to understand the unique skills and strengths of each team member. Assign tasks that align with individual capabilities, ensuring a well-rounded and competent crew. Just as a captain optimizes crew performance, your leadership optimizes team effectiveness by aligning tasks with individual strengths.

Strategic Task Alignment with Organizational Goals:
- A captain aligns crew tasks with the ship's overall goals. Leaders align individual tasks with the organization's objectives to ensure cohesive progress.
- Regularly revisit organizational goals and assess how individual tasks contribute to their achievement. Ensure that every team member's responsibilities align with the broader mission. Like a captain steering the ship toward a destination, your leadership guides the team toward organizational success through strategic task alignment.

Ensuring Crew Cohesion and Collaboration:
- A captain fosters collaboration among the crew for seamless operations. Leaders should encourage collaboration among team members to enhance overall productivity.
- Promote teamwork and cross-functional collaboration. Assign tasks that require different strengths, fostering a sense of interdependence. Just as a captain emphasizes teamwork for smooth sailing, your leadership creates a collaborative environment where individual strengths complement each other.

Recognizing and Celebrating Individual Achievements:
- A captain acknowledges the accomplishments of individual crew members. Similarly, leaders should recognize and celebrate the achievements of team members based on their assigned tasks.
- Establish a culture of appreciation by acknowledging individual contributions. Celebrate milestones and successes to boost morale and motivation. Like a captain recognizing the crew's efforts, your leadership ensures that individual achievements contribute to the overall success of the organization.

Empowering Team Members in Their Roles:
- A captain empowers crew members to excel in their roles. Leaders should empower team members by providing the necessary resources and support to excel in their assigned tasks.
- Identify and address any challenges that may hinder team members from performing at their best. Provide training and development opportunities to enhance skills. Similar to a captain empowering the crew, your leadership empowers individuals to excel in their assigned roles.

Dynamic Adjustment of Roles for Optimal Performance:
- A captain may adjust crew roles for optimal performance. Leaders should be open to adjusting team roles dynamically to optimize performance.

- Regularly assess team dynamics and adjust roles based on evolving needs and strengths. Be flexible in optimizing the team's structure for maximum efficiency. Just as a captain adjusts crew roles for optimal sailing, your leadership ensures that tasks are dynamically assigned to achieve the highest levels of performance.

Trusting your team.

Much like a captain relies on the competence and collaboration of their crew, effective leaders with the Captain Mariner Mindset understand the paramount importance of trust within a team. This analogical guide explores how cultivating trust among team members is a foundational element for smooth sailing in the realm of effective management.

Captain's Crew Trust:
- A captain places trust in the abilities of their crew. Similarly, leaders must trust the capabilities and commitment of their team members.
- Foster a culture of trust by recognizing and appreciating the skills and expertise of each team member. Delegate responsibilities based on trust in their abilities. Much like a captain trusts the crew for the ship's success, your leadership relies on the competence and dedication of your team for organizational achievements.

Aligning Trust with Organizational Goals:
- A captain trusts the crew to work towards the ship's destination.
  Leaders align trust with the organization's goals, entrusting team members to contribute to the overarching mission.
- Clearly communicate organizational goals and expectations, instilling confidence in your team's ability to achieve them. Trust team members to align their efforts with the broader vision. Similar to a captain entrusting the crew with the ship's journey, your leadership trusts the team to navigate towards organizational success.

Open Communication as the Compass of Trust:
- A captain communicates openly with the crew. Leaders must prioritize open communication as the compass of trust within the team.
- Encourage transparent and honest communication. Provide a platform for team members to express ideas, concerns, and feedback openly. Just as a captain communicates effectively for seamless sailing, your leadership ensures that open communication becomes the guiding principle of trust within the team.

Acknowledging Individual Strengths:
- A captain acknowledges the unique strengths of each crew member.
  Leaders should recognize and appreciate the individual strengths of team members, fostering a culture of trust and respect.
- Celebrate and leverage the diverse strengths within the team. Trust that each member brings valuable skills to the table, contributing to the collective success. Like a captain appreciates the crew's unique capabilities, your leadership values and trusts the distinct strengths of team members.

Empowering Decision-Making and Autonomy:
- A captain empowers the crew to make decisions autonomously. Leaders should empower team members by trusting them with decision-making authority and autonomy.
- Delegate decision-making responsibilities and empower team members to take ownership of their tasks. Trust their judgment and encourage a sense of responsibility. Similar to a captain empowering the crew, your leadership trusts team members to navigate and make decisions in their respective roles.

Balancing workload effectively.

Similar to a captain distributing tasks among the crew to ensure a well-balanced ship, effective leaders with the Captain Mariner Mindset understand the significance of balancing workload effectively. This analogical guide explores how distributing tasks strategically and considering team capacities contributes to smooth sailing in the realm of effective management.

Captain's Crew Task Allocation:

- A captain assigns tasks to ensure each crew member contributes to the ship's operation. Leaders must allocate tasks strategically to harness the collective strengths of their team.
- Assess the strengths and expertise of each team member. Distribute tasks based on individual capabilities, ensuring a well-rounded and efficient team. Like a captain optimizing crew performance, your leadership optimizes productivity by aligning tasks with individual strengths.

Strategic Task Distribution for Team Harmony:

- A captain distributes tasks to maintain harmony among the crew. Leaders distribute tasks strategically to foster a harmonious work environment.
- Consider team dynamics and workload capacities when assigning tasks. Distribute responsibilities in a way that promotes collaboration and prevents burnout. Much like a captain maintains crew harmony for smooth sailing, your leadership ensures a balanced workload for team synergy.

Prioritizing and Sequencing Tasks like Navigational Points:

- A captain navigates through predefined points. Leaders prioritize and sequence tasks strategically, creating a roadmap for optimal productivity.
- Establish clear priorities and sequences for tasks, aligning them with organizational goals. Ensure that each task contributes to the overall journey's success. Like a captain navigates through defined points, your leadership guides the team through tasks that lead to organizational success.

Monitoring Workload Buoyancy:

- A captain monitors the ship's buoyancy to ensure stability.
  Leaders monitor workload buoyancy by regularly assessing team capacity and adjusting task assignments.
- Stay vigilant to signs of potential overload within the team. Adjust task assignments based on workload and individual capacity to maintain stability. Similar to a captain ensuring the ship's buoyancy, your leadership safeguards team well-being by managing workload effectively.

Encouraging Open Communication about Workload:

- A captain encourages open communication among the crew. Leaders foster a culture of open communication about workload, ensuring team members feel comfortable expressing their capacity.
- Create an environment where team members feel safe discussing their workload and potential challenges. Address concerns promptly and adjust task assignments accordingly. Like a captain values open communication for smooth operations, your leadership ensures that workload discussions contribute to a healthy work environment.

Chapter **7**

Communication Onboard
Active listening and clear communication.

Much like a captain relies on effective communication and active listening to navigate the ship through unpredictable waters, leaders with the Captain Mariner Mindset understand the importance of clear communication and active listening in steering their teams toward success. This analogical guide explores how these practices contribute to smooth sailing in the realm of effective management.

Captain's Nautical Communication:
- A captain communicates vital information to the crew using nautical language. Leaders should adopt clear and concise communication methods to convey essential information.
- Develop a communication style that is straightforward and easily understandable. Avoid unnecessary complexity and jargon to ensure that the team receives messages clearly. Just as a captain communicates effectively for smooth sailing, your leadership communicates in a way that guides the team with clarity.

Navigating Through the Seas of Understanding:
- A captain navigates the ship by understanding navigational charts. Leaders navigate through challenges by fostering understanding through effective communication.
- Use communication as a navigational tool to guide the team through challenges. Clearly articulate goals, expectations, and strategies, fostering a shared understanding among team members. Like a captain understands navigational charts, your leadership ensures that the team comprehends the organizational direction.

Active Listening as the Compass of Leadership:
- A captain relies on a compass for direction. Leaders should use active listening as their compass, providing direction and understanding within the team.
- Practice active listening by giving full attention to team members, asking clarifying questions, and providing feedback. Use the insights gained to make informed decisions and guide the team effectively. Similar to a captain relying on a compass, your leadership uses active listening to navigate the team in the right direction.

Crew Briefings for Clarity:
- A captain conducts crew briefings for important information. Leaders should hold regular team briefings to convey important updates and ensure everyone is on the same page.
- Schedule regular team meetings to share updates, discuss goals, and address concerns. Provide a platform for open communication and encourage team members to ask questions. Like a captain conducts crew briefings, your leadership ensures that the team is well-informed and aligned.

Seamless Communication Channels:
- A captain ensures seamless communication between crew members. Leaders establish efficient communication channels to facilitate seamless information flow within the team.
- Implement tools and processes that enable efficient communication. Foster an environment where team members feel comfortable sharing information and ideas. Much like a captain ensures seamless communication on the ship, your leadership establishes channels that keep information flowing smoothly within the organization.

Navigating Through Stormy Communication Waters:
- A captain navigates through stormy weather with caution. Leaders should navigate through challenging communication situations with patience and a strategic approach.

- Approach difficult conversations with empathy and a focus on resolution. Address conflicts promptly and provide constructive feedback to maintain a positive communication environment. Similar to a captain navigating through stormy weather, your leadership navigates through challenging communication waters with resilience and skill.

Tools for effective team communication.
Comparable to a captain depending on progressed devices to communicate effectively with the team, successful pioneers with the Captain Sailor Attitude get it the significance of utilizing apparatuses for compelling group communication. This analogical direct investigates how utilizing communication instruments contributes to smooth cruising within the domain of viable administration.

Captain's Nautical Instruments:
- A captain uses nautical instruments for precise navigation. Leaders employ advanced communication tools as their instruments to ensure precise and efficient team collaboration.
- Identify and implement communication tools that suit the needs of the team. Whether it's project management software, messaging apps, or video conferencing tools, use them strategically to enhance communication and coordination. Similar to a captain relying on nautical instruments, your leadership leverages communication tools for accurate and efficient team navigation.

Charting a Digital Course:
- A captain charts a course on a navigational chart. Leaders chart a digital course for effective communication by selecting appropriate tools.
- Develop a digital communication strategy that includes tools for various purposes—project management, real-time messaging, virtual collaboration. Ensure that the chosen tools align with the organization's goals and facilitate efficient communication. Like a captain charts a course, your leadership charts a digital course for seamless communication within the team.

Sailing with Cloud-Based Collaboration:
- A captain utilizes weather data from the cloud for informed decisions. Leaders harness cloud-based collaboration tools to access and share information in real-time.
- Implement cloud-based tools for collaborative document sharing, project management, and data storage. This ensures that information is accessible to team members anytime, anywhere, fostering seamless collaboration. Similar to a captain utilizing weather data from the cloud, your leadership relies on cloud-based collaboration tools for informed decision-making.

Navigating the Seas of Real-Time Messaging:
- A captain uses radio communication for real-time updates. Leaders leverage real-time messaging tools to facilitate quick and efficient communication within the team.
- Integrate messaging apps that allow team members to communicate instantly. This enhances responsiveness, enables quick decision-making, and fosters a sense of real-time collaboration. Like a captain uses radio communication for instant updates, your leadership ensures real-time messaging tools keep the team connected.

Anchoring Virtual Meetings for Connection:
- A captain conducts ship briefings for important updates. Leaders anchor virtual meetings as essential gatherings to share updates, discuss goals, and foster team connection.
- Schedule regular virtual meetings to maintain face-to-face communication, even in remote work settings. This provides a platform for team briefings, collaborative discussions, and relationship-building. Much like a captain conducts ship briefings, your leadership anchors virtual meetings as crucial communication points.

Addressing communication barriers.

Just as a captain navigates through challenges to maintain open communication with the crew, effective leaders with the Captain Mariner Mindset understand the importance of addressing communication barriers to ensure smooth sailing in the realm of effective management. This analogical guide explores how leaders can clear the waters of communication obstacles to foster positive waves within their teams.

Captain's Skillful Maneuvers in Turbulent Waters:
- A captain skillfully maneuvers the ship through rough seas. Leaders navigate through communication barriers with skill and finesse to maintain effective team communication.
- Identify potential communication obstacles and develop strategies to navigate through them. Whether it's addressing misunderstandings or conflicts, approach communication challenges with a proactive and skillful mindset. Like a captain skillfully maneuvers through turbulent waters, your leadership navigates through communication barriers with resilience.

Navigational Chart of Transparent Communication:
- A captain relies on clear navigational charts for guidance. Leaders use transparent communication as their navigational chart, providing clear direction and avoiding ambiguity.
- Foster a culture of transparent communication by being clear and concise in your messages. Encourage openness and honesty within the team, ensuring that information flows smoothly without obstacles. Similar to a captain relying on navigational charts, your leadership uses transparent communication as a guide for effective team collaboration.

Steering Clear of Assumptions and Misinterpretations:
- A captain avoids assumptions and misinterpretations to navigate accurately. Leaders steer clear of assumptions and misinterpretations by ensuring clarity in communication.
- Encourage team members to seek clarification when uncertain and avoid making assumptions. Clearly articulate expectations and verify that messages are understood as intended. Much like a captain avoids assumptions, your leadership ensures a clear communication path by addressing potential misinterpretations.

Clearing the Fog of Poorly Defined Roles:
- A captain clears foggy conditions for improved visibility. Leaders clear the fog of poorly defined roles to enhance visibility and understanding within the team.
- Define and communicate team roles clearly to avoid confusion. Ensure that each team member understands their responsibilities and how they contribute to the overall mission. Like a captain clears fog for better visibility, your leadership clarifies roles to enhance understanding and collaboration.

Navigating Through Language and Cultural Differences:
- A captain navigates through diverse seas with different conditions. Leaders navigate through language and cultural differences, ensuring effective communication in diverse teams.
- Foster an inclusive environment that values diversity. Provide training on cross-cultural communication to enhance understanding. Consider language barriers and encourage open discussions to bridge gaps. Similar to a captain navigating diverse seas, your leadership navigates through diversity, addressing language and cultural differences for effective communication.

Chapter **8**

Conflict on the Deck
Recognizing the signs of conflict.

Within the tremendous oceans of successful administration, clashes can emerge like stormy climate. Pioneers with the Captain Sailor Attitude get it the significance of recognizing the signs of struggle early on. Comparative to a captain detecting the unobtrusive shifts within the wind or waves, pioneers can explore through organizational challenges by recognizing strife markers. This analogical direct investigates how recognizing these signs contributes to smooth cruising within the domain of compelling administration.

Captain's Weather Forecasting:
- A captain relies on weather forecasts to anticipate storms. Leaders use conflict indicators as a forecasting tool to anticipate potential organizational storms.
- Develop the ability to read subtle cues and changes in team dynamics. Pay attention to shifts in communication patterns, tension, or decreased collaboration. Just as a captain anticipates storms, your leadership uses conflict indicators to forecast potential challenges.

Navigating the Turbulent Waters of Miscommunication:
- A captain navigates through turbulent waters caused by miscommunication. Leaders navigate through organizational turbulence by addressing signs of miscommunication.
- Actively listen to team members, seek clarification when needed, and encourage open communication. Address any misunderstandings promptly to prevent them from escalating. Similar to a captain navigating through turbulent waters, your leadership navigates through miscommunication challenges to maintain a smooth course.

Monitoring Changes in Team Morale as Tides:
- A captain monitors changes in tides for navigation. Leaders monitor changes in team morale as an indicator of potential conflicts.
- Regularly assess team morale through surveys, feedback sessions, or informal check-ins. Sudden drops in morale may signal underlying conflicts that need attention. Like a captain monitors tides for navigation, your leadership monitors changes in team morale for effective conflict management.

Identifying Lingering Unresolved Issues as Storm Clouds:
- A captain identifies storm clouds on the horizon. Leaders identify lingering unresolved issues as potential storm clouds in the organizational landscape.
- Stay vigilant for unresolved issues that linger beneath the surface. Address conflicts promptly and encourage open discussions to prevent them from escalating. Much like a captain identifies storm clouds, your leadership identifies unresolved issues and addresses them before they intensify.

Listening to the Thunderous Silence of Disengagement:
- A captain listens for thunderous silence before a storm. Leaders listen for signs of disengagement among team members as a precursor to potential conflicts.
- Pay attention to team members who become disengaged or silent during discussions. This may indicate underlying concerns or disagreements that need addressing. Similar to a captain listening for thunderous silence, your leadership listens for signs of disengagement to proactively address conflicts.

Navigating the Choppy Waters of Interpersonal Strain:
- A captain navigates through choppy waters caused by crosscurrents.
Leaders navigate through organizational challenges arising from interpersonal strain within the team.

- Recognize signs of tension or strain between team members. Address interpersonal conflicts promptly and mediate when necessary to maintain a cohesive team. Like a captain navigates choppy waters, your leadership navigates through interpersonal strain for smooth collaboration.

Strategies for conflict resolution.

Just as a captain navigates through storms at sea, effective leaders with the Captain Mariner Mindset understand the importance of implementing strategies for conflict resolution to maintain smooth sailing within their teams. This analogical guide explores how adopting conflict resolution strategies contributes to effective management and creates positive waves in the organizational seas.

Captain's Navigation Charts for Conflict Resolution:
- A captain uses navigation charts to navigate through stormy waters. Leaders develop conflict resolution strategies as their navigation charts for steering through organizational challenges.
- Establish a set of predefined conflict resolution strategies, outlining steps to address different types of conflicts. Equip the team with these "navigation charts" to guide them through stormy situations. Similar to a captain using navigation charts, your leadership relies on conflict resolution strategies for effective problem-solving.

Setting the Course for Open Dialogue:
- A captain encourages open dialogue among the crew during challenges. Leaders set the course for open dialogue as a fundamental strategy for conflict resolution.
- Foster an environment where team members feel comfortable expressing concerns and engaging in open discussions. Encourage active listening and provide a platform for constructive dialogue. Much like a captain promotes open dialogue, your leadership sets the course for transparent communication in conflict resolution.

Utilizing Mediation as the Crew Mediator:
- A captain may act as a mediator between conflicting crew members. Leaders use formal mediation as a strategy to resolve conflicts within the team.
- Train designated mediators within the team or involve HR professionals when conflicts escalate. Mediation can help parties find common ground and reach resolutions. Like a captain mediating between crew members, your leadership utilizes mediation as an effective strategy for conflict resolution.

Navigating Through Compromise Like Maneuvering Through Rocks:
- A captain maneuvers through rocky waters with compromise. Leaders navigate through conflicts by encouraging compromise as a key strategy for resolution.
- Emphasize the importance of finding middle ground and making concessions to resolve conflicts. Encourage team members to seek win-win solutions. Similar to a captain navigating through rocks with compromise, your leadership navigates through conflicts by promoting compromise.

Hoisting the Flag of Collaboration:
- A captain signals collaboration during challenging times. Leaders hoist the flag of collaboration as a strategy to resolve conflicts and foster teamwork.
- Emphasize the collective goals and the importance of working together. Encourage collaborative problem-solving to find solutions that benefit the entire team. Much like a captain signals collaboration, your leadership promotes a collaborative spirit as a strategy for conflict resolution.

The positive side of conflict.

Much like a captain who navigates through storms at sea, effective leaders with the Captain Mariner Mindset recognize that conflict, when approached with the right perspective, can have positive outcomes. This analogical guide explores the positive side of conflict and how, with strategic navigation, leaders can harness these storms for organizational growth and create positive waves in the seas of effective management.

Captain's Perspective on Storms as Catalysts for Change:

- A captain sees storms as catalysts for change, forcing the ship to adapt and grow. Leaders view conflicts as opportunities for positive change and growth within the organization.
- Encourage a mindset that sees conflicts as natural occurrences that can spur innovation and improvement. Emphasize the potential for positive change that arises from addressing and resolving conflicts. Much like a captain viewing storms as catalysts, your leadership recognizes conflicts as catalysts for positive organizational transformation.

Navigating the Waters of Differing Perspectives:

- A captain navigates through waters where different currents meet. Leaders navigate through conflicts by embracing diverse perspectives and leveraging them for innovation.
- Encourage open discussions that allow team members to express diverse viewpoints. Use conflicts as opportunities to explore new ideas and perspectives, fostering a culture of innovation. Similar to a captain navigating through different currents, your leadership navigates through conflicts by embracing and leveraging diverse perspectives.

Fostering a Culture of Continuous Improvement:

- A captain continuously improves the ship's performance based on challenges faced. Leaders foster a culture of continuous improvement by using conflicts as feedback for refining processes and strategies.
- Encourage teams to reflect on conflicts and identify areas for improvement. Implement changes based on lessons learned from resolving conflicts, promoting a culture of continuous enhancement. Like a captain improving ship performance, your leadership uses conflict resolution as a means for organizational refinement.

Harvesting Innovation in the Wake of Conflict:

- A captain explores uncharted territories after storms, discovering new routes. Leaders harness innovation in the wake of conflict, exploring uncharted territories for organizational advancement.
- Encourage creative problem-solving during conflict resolution. Use conflicts as opportunities to identify innovative solutions that can enhance processes and contribute to organizational growth. Much like a captain exploring new routes after storms, your leadership explores new avenues for innovation in the aftermath of conflict.

Strengthening Team Bonds Through Adversity:

- A captain's crew bonds through shared adversity during storms. Leaders strengthen team bonds by navigating through conflicts together, fostering resilience and unity.
- Encourage teamwork during conflict resolution, emphasizing the collective effort required to overcome challenges. Team members can emerge stronger and more connected after navigating through conflicts together. Like a captain's crew bonding through adversity, your leadership strengthens team bonds through shared experiences in conflict resolution.

Chapter **9**

Sailing Through Storms
Crisis management.

In the unpredictable seas of organizational management, crises can emerge like sudden storms. Leaders with the Captain Mariner Mindset understand the crucial role of crisis management in steering their teams through uncertainty. This analogical guide explores how effective crisis management, akin to a captain's response to tempestuous conditions, contributes to maintaining smooth sailing and creating positive waves in the realm of effective leadership.

Captain's Preparedness for Unexpected Storms:
- A captain maintains preparedness for unexpected storms. Leaders approach crisis management with proactive planning and readiness for unforeseen challenges.
- Develop comprehensive crisis management plans that encompass various potential scenarios. Regularly update these plans, ensuring the team is well-prepared to navigate through crises effectively. Similar to a captain's preparedness for storms, your leadership maintains readiness for unexpected challenges.

Navigating the Turbulent Seas of Crisis Communication:
- A captain communicates clearly during turbulent conditions. Leaders practice effective crisis communication, ensuring transparent and timely information dissemination.
- Establish a clear communication protocol for crises, outlining roles, responsibilities, and channels of communication. Prioritize transparency to maintain trust and keep the team informed during turbulent times. Much like a captain communicates during turbulence, your leadership navigates through crisis communication with clarity and transparency.

Utilizing Crisis as a Course Correction Opportunity:
- A captain may need to adjust the ship's course during crises. Leaders view crises as opportunities for course correction and strategic refinement.
- Assess the root causes of crises and use them as valuable feedback for organizational improvement. Implement necessary changes to enhance resilience and mitigate future risks. Like a captain adjusting the ship's course, your leadership utilizes crises for strategic course correction.

Maintaining Steady Leadership Amidst Storms:
- A captain maintains composure and steady leadership during storms. Leaders exhibit calm and steadfast leadership to instill confidence in the team during crises.
- Stay composed, provide reassurance, and demonstrate a steady hand in decision-making during crises. Instill confidence in the team by showcasing resilience and a commitment to overcoming challenges. Similar to a captain maintaining composure, your leadership provides steady guidance through turbulent times.

Charting a Course for Recovery and Resilience:
- A captain charts a course for recovery after a storm. Leaders chart a course for organizational recovery and resilience, emphasizing lessons learned from crises.
- Develop post-crisis recovery plans that focus on rebuilding and reinforcing organizational resilience. Use the experience to strengthen processes, identify vulnerabilities, and ensure preparedness for future challenges. Like a captain charting a course for recovery, your leadership guides the organization toward resilience after crises.

Learning from Crisis as Nautical Wisdom:
- A captain learns from each crisis to refine navigation strategies. Leaders extract valuable lessons from crises, applying them to improve organizational strategies and decision-making.
- Conduct thorough post-crisis assessments to identify successes and areas for improvement. Use these insights to enhance crisis management plans and organizational resilience. Much like a captain learning from crises, your leadership applies nautical wisdom to refine strategies for effective crisis management.

Maintaining composure under pressure.

Like a captain who remains composed in the face of tumultuous seas, effective leaders with the Captain Mariner Mindset understand the importance of maintaining composure under pressure. This analogical guide explores how keeping a steady hand during challenging times contributes to smooth sailing in the realm of effective management and creates positive waves within the organizational waters.

Captain's Steadfast Presence in the Storm:
- A captain maintains a steadfast presence on the ship during storms. Leaders emulate this by being a steady presence for their teams during challenging and high-pressure situations.
- Demonstrate calmness and resilience in the face of adversity. Your composed demeanor sets the tone for the team, instilling confidence and reinforcing stability amidst uncertainty. Like a captain's steadfast presence, your leadership provides a reliable anchor for the team during storms.

Navigating Through Choppy Waters with Poise:
- A captain navigates through choppy waters with poise. Leaders navigate through challenging times with poise, showcasing grace under pressure.
- Cultivate the ability to make decisions thoughtfully and effectively under pressure. Maintain a level-headed approach to problem-solving, inspiring confidence in the team that can weather any storm. Similar to a captain navigating through choppy waters, your leadership navigates through challenges with poise.

Inspiring Confidence Through Resilience:
- A captain's resilience inspires confidence in the crew. Leaders inspire confidence through their own resilience, showing the team that challenges can be overcome.
- Embrace setbacks as opportunities to showcase resilience. Demonstrate adaptability and a positive outlook, reinforcing the belief that the team can face and conquer challenges together. Much like a captain's resilience inspiring the crew, your leadership's resilience inspires confidence in the team.

Communicating Calmly in the Eye of the Storm:
- A captain communicates calmly in the eye of the storm.
  Leaders communicate with a calm and steady demeanor, providing reassurance to the team during turbulent times.
- Practice effective communication that conveys reassurance and stability. Clearly articulate plans and decisions, ensuring that the team feels informed and supported. Like a captain communicating in the eye of the storm, your leadership communicates calmly amidst challenges.

Strategic Decision-Making as Navigation:
- A captain makes strategic decisions to navigate safely. Leaders make strategic decisions as a form of navigation through pressure, ensuring the team reaches safe harbor.
- When under pressure, focus on making well-thought-out decisions that consider both short-term and long-term implications. Lead with strategic vision, steering the team

towards success even in challenging conditions. Similar to a captain making strategic decisions, your leadership strategically navigates through pressure.

Leading through adversity.

In the expanse of organizational waters, effective leaders with the Captain Mariner Mindset understand the critical role of leading through adversity. Similar to a captain steering a ship through challenging conditions, this analogical guide explores how effective leadership in the face of adversity contributes to smooth sailing, creating positive waves within the organizational landscape.

Captain's Resolute Helm in Stormy Seas:
- A captain remains resolute at the helm during stormy seas. Leaders embody this by standing firm in their role, steering the team through adversity with determination.
- Embrace challenges as opportunities to demonstrate resilience and determination. Your steadfast leadership at the helm inspires the team, showing them that they can navigate through stormy seas under your guidance. Similar to a captain's resolute helm, your leadership stands firm in the face of adversity.

Navigating Through the Fog of Uncertainty:
- A captain navigates through the fog, relying on experience and instruments. Leaders navigate through uncertainty by leveraging experience and strategic guidance.
- Provide clear direction and guidance during uncertain times. Rely on your experience and the insights of the team to chart a course through the fog of challenges, ensuring everyone is moving in the right direction. Like a captain navigating through the fog, your leadership guides the team through uncertain waters.

Staying the Course in the Face of Setbacks:
- A captain stays the course despite setbacks. Leaders stay committed to the organizational course, even when facing setbacks, demonstrating resilience.
- In the face of setbacks, communicate a sense of purpose and commitment to the team. Showcase adaptability and determination, reinforcing the belief that the team can overcome obstacles together. Similar to a captain staying the course, your leadership remains committed to the organizational mission despite challenges.

Inspiring Hope as the North Star:
- A captain's leadership becomes the guiding North Star for the crew. Leaders inspire hope by becoming the beacon of guidance and assurance during challenging times.
- Communicate a positive vision for the future, emphasizing the team's ability to overcome adversity. Your leadership becomes the North Star, providing hope and direction, guiding the team through the darkness of challenges. Like a captain's leadership as the North Star, your leadership inspires hope and assurance.

Delegating Effectively as Crew Coordination:
- A captain coordinates the crew during challenges. Leaders delegate effectively, ensuring the team collaborates efficiently to navigate through adversity.
- Identify strengths within the team and delegate responsibilities accordingly. Foster collaboration and open communication to enhance collective problem-solving. Much like a captain coordinating the crew, your leadership ensures effective delegation for optimal teamwork during adversity.

Chapter **10**

Steering Towards Motivation
Intrinsic vs. extrinsic motivation.

Understanding the dynamics of motivation is akin to navigating through currents. Leaders with the Captain Mariner Mindset comprehend the distinction between intrinsic and extrinsic motivation, essential for steering their teams towards smooth sailing. This analogical guide explores the intrinsic and extrinsic currents of motivation, illuminating how effective management harnesses both to create positive waves within the organizational landscape.

Intrinsic Motivation: The Wind in the Sails of Passion:
- Intrinsic motivation is like the wind that fills the sails of passion. Just as a captain harnesses the wind's natural force to propel the ship forward, leaders cultivate intrinsic motivation to fuel their team's passion and drive.
- Encourage autonomy, mastery, and purpose within the team, fostering a sense of ownership and fulfillment in their work.
  Provide opportunities for personal growth and development, allowing team members to pursue their passions and interests. Like a captain harnessing the wind, your leadership harnesses intrinsic motivation to propel the team forward with passion and purpose.

Extrinsic Motivation: The Rudder of Recognition and Rewards:
- Extrinsic motivation serves as the rudder that steers the ship towards desired destinations. Leaders utilize recognition and rewards as the rudder of extrinsic motivation, guiding the team towards achieving organizational goals.
- Offer tangible rewards, such as bonuses or incentives, to recognize and reinforce desired behaviors and achievements. Provide praise and acknowledgment for exemplary performance, highlighting the value of contributions to the team and organization. Similar to a captain using the rudder to steer the ship, your leadership uses extrinsic motivation to guide the team towards success.

Balancing the Motivational Tides:
- Effective navigation requires balancing the forces of wind and rudder. Similarly, effective management entails balancing intrinsic and extrinsic motivation to optimize team performance.
- Recognize that different individuals may be motivated by different factors, and strive to create a balance between intrinsic and extrinsic motivators within the team. Tailor motivational strategies to individual preferences and circumstances, ensuring alignment with overarching organizational goals. Like a captain balancing the forces of wind and rudder, your leadership balances intrinsic and extrinsic motivation to navigate towards success.

Cultivating a Culture of Intrinsic Fulfillment:
- A captain fosters a culture where sailors find fulfillment in the journey itself. Leaders cultivate a culture where team members derive intrinsic fulfillment from the work they do and the goals they pursue.
- Foster a sense of purpose and meaning within the team by aligning organizational objectives with individual values and aspirations. Create opportunities for meaningful contributions and impactful work, empowering team members to find fulfillment in their roles. Much like a captain fostering a culture of fulfillment, your leadership cultivates intrinsic motivation within the team.

Harnessing Extrinsic Motivation as a Guiding Beacon:
- A captain uses the lighthouse as a guiding beacon in the darkness. Leaders utilize extrinsic motivation as a guiding beacon, providing clear direction and incentives to steer the team towards shared objectives.
- Set clear goals and expectations, offering rewards and recognition as milestones are achieved. Use extrinsic motivators strategically to reinforce desired behaviors and outcomes, keeping the team focused and aligned with organizational priorities. Similar to a captain using the lighthouse as a guiding beacon, your leadership utilizes extrinsic motivation to guide the team towards success.

Adapting to Changing Motivational Currents:
- Effective navigation requires adjusting course in response to changing currents. Similarly, effective management entails adapting motivational strategies in response to evolving team dynamics and objectives.
- Stay attuned to the motivational needs of the team, regularly assessing and adjusting motivational strategies as necessary. Be flexible and responsive to changes in individual preferences, performance levels, and external circumstances, ensuring continued engagement and commitment.

Rewards and recognition systems.

Effective leaders with the Captain Mariner Mindset understand the importance of Rewards and Recognition Systems as essential navigation tools. Similar to a captain acknowledging and rewarding the efforts of their crew, this analogical guide explores how a well-structured system of rewards and recognition contributes to smooth sailing, creating positive waves within the organizational landscape.

Captain's Log of Achievement:
- A captain maintains a log of the crew's achievements. Leaders keep a metaphorical "Captain's Log" of accomplishments through a Rewards and Recognition System, documenting and celebrating the successes of the team.
- Implement a systematic approach to record and acknowledge individual and team achievements. Maintain a visible record of accomplishments, showcasing the collective progress and fostering a sense of pride within the team. Much like a captain's log, your Rewards and Recognition System becomes a testament to the journey and triumphs of the team.

Treasure Chest of Incentives:
- A captain treasures the spoils of successful voyages. Leaders establish a "Treasure Chest" of incentives within the Rewards and Recognition System, offering tangible rewards as treasures for outstanding contributions.
- Create a range of incentives, such as bonuses, gift cards, or special perks, to motivate and reward exceptional performance. This Treasure Chest becomes a symbol of appreciation and a source of motivation, encouraging the team to strive for excellence. Like a captain treasuring the spoils, your leadership values and rewards the fruits of hard work.

Navigating the Waters of Individualized Recognition:
- A captain recognizes each crew member's unique contributions. Leaders navigate through the waters of individualized recognition, tailoring acknowledgment to highlight the distinct achievements and strengths of each team member.
- Personalize recognition efforts to align with the individual preferences and aspirations of team members. Acknowledge specific accomplishments, skills, or milestones, creating a culture of appreciation that values the uniqueness of each contributor.

Similar to a captain recognizing each crew member, your leadership embraces individuality in recognition.

Guiding Beacons of Public Praise:
- A captain's praise is like guiding beacons for the crew. Leaders use public praise as guiding beacons within the Rewards and Recognition System, illuminating exemplary efforts for the entire team to see.
- Celebrate achievements openly, whether through team meetings, newsletters, or dedicated recognition events. Publicly acknowledge outstanding performance to not only commend individuals but also inspire others to strive for excellence. Like a captain's guiding beacons, public praise lights the way for continuous success.

Creating an environment that fosters self-motivation.

In the expansive realm of organizational waters, effective leaders with the Captain Mariner Mindset understand the importance of cultivating an environment that fosters self-motivation. Much like a captain empowering the crew to take initiative, this analogical guide explores how creating a self-motivated environment contributes to smooth sailing, generating positive waves within the organizational landscape.

The Captain's Call to Adventure:
- A captain inspires the crew with the promise of exciting adventures. Leaders, like captains, ignite the spark of self-motivation by presenting work as an exhilarating journey filled with opportunities and challenges.
- Communicate a compelling vision for the team, emphasizing the meaningful impact of their work. Frame tasks and projects as exciting adventures, encouraging team members to take ownership and initiative. Like a captain's call to adventure, your leadership inspires self-motivation through a shared vision of exciting possibilities.

Empowering Crew Autonomy Like a Sail in the Wind:
- A captain trusts the crew to set sail independently. Leaders empower their teams with autonomy, allowing them to navigate their own course and find motivation as the wind fills their sails.
- Delegate responsibilities and grant autonomy to team members, trusting them to make decisions and contribute independently. Provide the necessary support and resources, allowing individuals to take ownership of their work and find motivation in accomplishing tasks autonomously. Similar to a captain empowering the crew, your leadership fosters self-motivation by allowing the team to set sail independently.

Navigating through Recognition Currents:
- A captain acknowledges the crew's contributions. Leaders navigate through recognition currents, offering timely and sincere acknowledgment to fuel the team's self-motivation.
- Regularly recognize and celebrate individual and team achievements. Acknowledge efforts and contributions publicly, creating a culture where self-motivation is fueled by the gratification of a job well done.

  Like a captain acknowledging the crew, your leadership fuels self-motivation through the currents of recognition.

Charting Personal Growth Courses:
- A captain invests in the crew's skill development. Leaders, like captains, chart courses for personal and professional growth, fostering self-motivation through continuous learning and advancement.
- Encourage skill development and provide opportunities for learning and growth. Support the team in setting personal and professional goals, aligning them with the organization's objectives. Much like a captain investing in the crew's skills, your leadership charts courses for individual growth, nurturing self-motivation.

Chapter **11**

Charting Progress
Performance management and evaluation.

Effective leaders with the Captain Mariner Mindset understand the crucial role of Performance Management and Evaluation as navigational tools. Similar to a captain steering the ship through waters with precision, this analogical guide explores how a well-crafted performance management system contributes to smooth sailing, creating positive waves within the organizational landscape.

The Navigation Chart of Expectations:
- A captain relies on navigation charts for a clear course. Leaders utilize a metaphorical "Navigation Chart of Expectations" within performance management, setting clear expectations and goals to guide the team toward success.
- Establish clear performance expectations and goals for individual team members. Define key performance indicators (KPIs) that align with organizational objectives, providing a roadmap for success. Like a captain relying on navigation charts, your leadership sets a clear course for excellence through performance expectations.

The Helm of Constructive Feedback:
- A captain adjusts the helm to navigate effectively. Leaders, too, adjust the helm through constructive feedback within the performance management system, steering the team towards improvement and success.
- Provide regular and constructive feedback on individual and team performance. Offer guidance for improvement and highlight areas of strength. The helm of constructive feedback ensures that the team sails in the right direction, making necessary course adjustments. Similar to a captain adjusting the helm, your leadership uses constructive feedback to navigate the team effectively.

The Lighthouse of Recognition and Rewards:
- A captain navigates by the light of a lighthouse. Leaders guide their teams with a metaphorical "Lighthouse of Recognition and Rewards" within performance management, offering acknowledgment and incentives as guiding beacons.
- Recognize and reward exceptional performance through a structured system. The lighthouse of recognition illuminates the path to success, motivating the team to strive for excellence.
  Much like a captain navigating by a lighthouse, your leadership uses recognition and rewards as guiding beacons in performance management.

Navigating Through Calm and Storm:
- A captain navigates through both calm and stormy seas. Leaders, too, navigate through the varying performance landscapes, ensuring effective management and evaluation in all conditions.
- Address performance challenges proactively and provide support during both calm and turbulent times. The ability to navigate through different performance scenarios ensures the team's resilience and adaptability. Similar to a captain navigating through various sea conditions, your leadership effectively manages performance in all situations.

The Logbook of Individual Growth:
- A captain maintains a logbook of the ship's journey.
  Leaders keep a metaphorical "Logbook of Individual Growth" within performance management, documenting the progress and development of each team member.
- Regularly assess and document individual growth and achievements.

Use the logbook to track performance trends and identify opportunities for professional development. Much like a captain's logbook, your leadership captures the journey of individual growth through performance management.

The Compass of Fair Evaluation:

- A captain relies on a compass for accurate direction. Leaders use the "Compass of Fair Evaluation" within performance management, ensuring impartial and objective assessments for all team members.
- Conduct evaluations with fairness and objectivity, considering individual contributions and achievements. The compass of fair evaluation guides decision-making and promotes a culture of transparency and accountability. Like a captain relying on a compass, your leadership ensures fair and accurate evaluations within the performance management system.

Feedback mechanisms.

Leaders with the Captain Mariner Mindset understand the importance of Feedback Mechanisms as compasses for course correction. Similar to a captain relying on feedback to navigate through changing conditions, this analogical guide explores how well-crafted feedback mechanisms contribute to smooth sailing, creating positive waves within the organizational landscape.

The Compass of Timely Feedback:

- A captain relies on a compass for real-time direction. Leaders use the "Compass of Timely Feedback" to provide direction and guidance promptly, ensuring the team navigates towards success with agility.
- Establish a system for timely feedback, offering insights and guidance as situations unfold. Like a captain relying on a compass for immediate direction, your leadership uses timely feedback to guide the team through dynamic organizational waters.

The Lighthouse of Constructive Critique:

- A captain navigates by the light of a lighthouse.
  Leaders use the "Lighthouse of Constructive Critique" within feedback mechanisms, offering constructive guidance as a guiding beacon for continuous improvement.
- Illuminate areas for improvement with constructive criticism, providing a clear path forward. The lighthouse of constructive critique ensures that the team sails towards excellence, using feedback as a guiding light. Similar to a captain navigating by a lighthouse, your leadership uses constructive critique as a guiding beacon within feedback mechanisms.

Navigating the Turbulent Seas of Challenges:

- A captain navigates through stormy seas. Leaders navigate the turbulent seas of challenges through feedback mechanisms, addressing issues proactively to ensure a smoother journey.
- Use feedback to address challenges promptly, guiding the team through rough patches with constructive solutions. The ability to navigate through turbulent seas of challenges ensures resilience and adaptability. Like a captain navigating through stormy seas, your leadership steers the team through challenges with effective feedback mechanisms.

The Sounding Horn of Encouragement:

- A captain uses a sounding horn to convey encouragement. Leaders use the "Sounding Horn of Encouragement" within feedback mechanisms, fostering a positive and motivated environment.
- Incorporate positive feedback and encouragement into the feedback process, recognizing and appreciating individual and team efforts. The sounding horn of encouragement motivates the team to continue their journey with enthusiasm. Much like a captain using a sounding horn, your leadership encourages the team with positive feedback within the feedback mechanisms.

Encouraging self-improvement and professional growth.

Leaders with the Captain Mariner Mindset recognize the importance of Encouraging Self-Improvement and Professional Growth as vital sails for organizational progress. Similar to a captain fostering the skill sets of their crew, this analogical guide explores how encouraging self-improvement and professional growth contributes to smooth sailing, creating positive waves within the organizational landscape.

The Compass of Individual Aspirations:

- A captain navigates by the compass to align with true north. Leaders utilize the "Compass of Individual Aspirations" to understand and align professional growth opportunities with each team member's unique goals.

- Engage in open discussions with team members to identify their aspirations and career goals. Use this compass to chart personalized professional growth plans, ensuring alignment with both individual aspirations and organizational objectives. Your leadership guides professional growth according to individual aspirations.

Sails of Skill Development:

- A captain adjusts the sails to harness the wind's power. Leaders adjust the "Sails of Skill Development" to harness the potential within each team member, promoting continuous learning and skill enhancement.

- Encourage ongoing skill development through training, workshops, and educational opportunities. Adjust the sails to match the winds of emerging industry trends, ensuring that the team is equipped with the latest skills needed for success. Similar to a captain adjusting sails, your leadership adapts skill development to navigate through dynamic professional landscapes.

Navigating Through Learning Currents:

- A captain navigates through currents to reach the destination. Leaders navigate through the "Learning Currents," ensuring that team members have access to resources that keep them updated and enhance their professional knowledge.

- Provide access to learning resources, mentorship programs, and industry insights. Navigate through learning currents by encouraging the team to explore new areas of expertise and stay abreast of industry developments.

  Like a captain navigating through currents, your leadership guides the team through learning opportunities for continuous professional growth.

The Lighthouse of Mentorship:

- A captain relies on the lighthouse for guidance. Leaders use the "Lighthouse of Mentorship" to provide guidance and support, helping team members navigate the often challenging waters of professional growth.

- Establish mentorship programs within the organization, pairing experienced individuals with those seeking guidance. The lighthouse of mentorship illuminates the path, offering valuable insights and support for individuals on their professional journeys. Much like a captain relying on a lighthouse, your leadership uses mentorship as a guiding light for professional growth.

Chapter **12**

Training Seafarers
Professional development opportunities.

In the expansive ocean of effective management, leaders with the Captain Mariner Mindset understand the significance of Professional Development Opportunities as essential sails for organizational progress. Similar to a captain charting courses for their crew's skill enhancement, this analogical guide explores how providing professional development opportunities contributes to smooth sailing, creating positive waves within the organizational landscape.

The Nautical Chart of Skill Enhancement:
- A captain relies on nautical charts for safe navigation. Leaders use the "Nautical Chart of Skill Enhancement" to identify and map professional development opportunities, ensuring the team navigates towards success with a clear path.
- Regularly assess the skill sets within the team and identify areas for improvement. Use the nautical chart to navigate through the sea of professional development options, aligning them with both individual growth needs and organizational objectives.
  Like a captain relying on nautical charts, your leadership charts courses for skill enhancement through professional development opportunities.

Adjusting Sails to Emerging Trends:
- A captain adjusts sails to harness favorable winds. Leaders adjust the "Sails to Emerging Trends" within professional development opportunities, ensuring that the team stays aligned with the latest industry trends and advancements.
- Stay informed about emerging trends in the industry and align professional development opportunities accordingly. Adjust the sails to harness the winds of innovation, keeping the team abreast of current and future needs. Similar to a captain adjusting sails, your leadership adapts to industry trends through well-aligned professional development opportunities.

The Navigation Beacon of Cross-Functional Training:
- A captain relies on navigation beacons for guidance. Leaders use the "Navigation Beacon of Cross-Functional Training" to guide the team towards versatility, offering opportunities for cross-functional skill development.
  Introduce cross-functional training programs to enhance the team's versatility and foster a more collaborative environment. The navigation beacon of cross-functional training guides the team towards a broader skill set, enriching their professional capabilities. Much like a captain relying on navigation beacons, your leadership uses cross-functional training as a guiding light within professional development opportunities.

Sailing the Open Waters of Conferences and Workshops:
- A captain sails the open waters for new horizons. Leaders encourage the team to sail the open waters of conferences and workshops, exposing them to new ideas, technologies, and perspectives.
- Support and sponsor team members to attend relevant conferences and workshops. Sailing the open waters of such events broadens their horizons and provides valuable insights, contributing to both personal and professional development. Like a captain exploring new horizons, your leadership encourages the team to sail through conferences and workshops for enriching professional experiences.

The Harbor of Mentoring Programs:
- A captain seeks shelter in a safe harbor. Leaders create a "Harbor of Mentoring Programs" within professional development opportunities, providing a safe space for guidance, support, and skill-sharing.
- Establish mentoring programs where seasoned professionals guide and share insights with less experienced team members. The harbor of mentoring programs offers a supportive environment for continuous learning, helping individuals navigate their professional journeys. Similar to a captain seeking shelter in a harbor, your leadership provides a secure space for growth through mentoring programs.

Navigating Through Online Learning Channels:
- A captain navigates using modern technology. Leaders guide the team through the online learning channels, ensuring that digital platforms are leveraged effectively for flexible and accessible professional development.
- : Embrace online learning platforms and e-courses to provide flexible learning opportunities. Navigate through the digital landscape, utilizing technology for continuous skill development that suits the diverse needs of the team.

Mentoring and coaching.

In the sea of effective management, leaders with the Captain Mariner Mindset recognize the crucial role of Mentoring and Coaching as guiding stars for organizational success. Similar to a captain mentoring and coaching the crew, this analogical guide explores how well-crafted mentoring and coaching strategies contribute to smooth sailing, creating positive waves within the organizational landscape.

The Captain's Mentorship Harbor:
- A captain mentors the crew through challenging waters. Leaders create a "Mentorship Harbor" within the organization, providing a safe space for team members to receive guidance and support.
- Establish formal mentorship programs or informal mentoring relationships where experienced individuals guide their peers or subordinates. The mentorship harbor ensures that team members have a reliable source of advice and encouragement as they navigate their professional journeys. Much like a captain mentoring through challenging waters, your leadership provides a mentorship harbor for continuous support and growth.

Coaching as the Compass of Improvement:
- A captain uses a compass to navigate accurately. Leaders use "Coaching as the Compass of Improvement," offering targeted guidance to help individuals find their professional direction.
- Implement coaching sessions to address specific skill development or performance improvement areas. The coaching compass ensures that individuals receive personalized guidance, steering them towards improvement and success. Similar to a captain using a compass for accuracy, your leadership employs coaching as a strategic tool for individual improvement.

Navigating the Waves of Skill Enhancement:
- A captain navigates through waves with skill and precision. Leaders navigate the waves of skill enhancement through mentoring and coaching, ensuring that team members continually develop and refine their abilities.
- Provide targeted coaching sessions to enhance specific skills required for individual roles. The navigation through skill enhancement waves ensures that the team is well-equipped to tackle challenges effectively.
  Like a captain navigating through waves with skill, your leadership guides the team through skill enhancement with mentoring and coaching.

The North Star of Professional Development:
- A captain uses the North Star for navigation. Leaders utilize "The North Star of Professional Development" through mentoring and coaching, offering a constant reference point for team members to align their professional journeys.
- Align mentoring and coaching programs with the overarching goals of professional development. The North Star ensures that team members have a consistent guiding light, facilitating continuous improvement and growth. Much like a captain relying on the North Star, your leadership provides a guiding light for professional development through mentoring and coaching.

Upskilling and reskilling.

In effective management, leaders with the Captain Mariner Mindset understand the importance of Upskilling and Reskilling as essential navigation tools. Similar to a captain ensuring the crew is adept at handling evolving conditions, this analogical guide explores how well-crafted upskilling and reskilling strategies contribute to smooth sailing, creating positive waves within the organizational landscape.

Charting the Course of Skill Evolution:
- A captain charts the course for the ship. Leaders, too, chart the course of skill evolution through Upskilling and Reskilling, ensuring that the team is equipped to navigate through changing industry landscapes.
- Conduct regular assessments of skill sets within the team and identify areas for enhancement. Chart a comprehensive course for upskilling and reskilling, aligning it with both individual aspirations and organizational needs.

Adapting Sails to Emerging Winds of Knowledge:
- A captain adjusts the sails for the changing wind. Leaders adjust the "Sails of Skill Development" in response to the emerging winds of knowledge, ensuring the team stays current and effective.
- Keep a vigilant eye on emerging industry trends and technologies. Adjust the sails of skill development to align with the changing winds, allowing the team to harness the power of new knowledge. Similar to a captain adjusting sails, your leadership adapts skill development to navigate through dynamic professional landscapes.

Navigating the Currents of Emerging Technologies:
- A captain navigates through currents for efficiency. Leaders navigate through the "Currents of Emerging Technologies," ensuring that the team is well-versed in the latest tools and technologies.
- Invest in training programs that expose the team to emerging technologies. Navigate through the currents of technological advancements, ensuring that the team remains efficient and competitive. Like a captain navigating currents, your leadership guides the team through technology adoption for enhanced effectiveness.

The Compass of Individual Skill Maps:
- A captain uses a compass for direction. Leaders use the "Compass of Individual Skill Maps" to understand each team member's current skills and future aspirations, ensuring personalized upskilling and reskilling plans.
- Conduct individual skill assessments and engage in open dialogues about career aspirations. Use the compass of individual skill maps to tailor upskilling and reskilling plans that align with both personal growth and organizational objectives. Much like a captain using a compass, your leadership navigates through personalized skill maps for effective skill development.

The Harbor of Learning and Development Programs:
- A captain seeks shelter in a harbor during storms. Leaders provide a "Harbor of Learning and Development Programs," offering a safe space for team members to enhance their skills and weather the storms of evolving job requirements.

- Establish robust learning and development programs within the organization. The harbor of learning and development programs ensures that team members have a secure space to acquire new skills and adapt to changing job demands.

Chapter **13**

Maintaining the Vessel
The importance of operational efficiency.

In the sea of effective management, leaders with the Captain Mariner Mindset recognize the paramount importance of Operational Efficiency as the rudder steering the ship of success. Similar to a captain ensuring the ship runs with precision, this analogical guide explores how prioritizing operational efficiency contributes to smooth sailing, creating positive waves within the organizational landscape.

The Rudder of Operational Efficiency:
- A captain relies on the rudder for precise navigation. Leaders utilize the "Rudder of Operational Efficiency" to steer the organization with accuracy and effectiveness.
- Implement streamlined processes, effective workflows, and optimized resource allocation to enhance operational efficiency. Like a captain relying on the rudder, your leadership ensures that the organization moves in the right direction with precision and purpose.

Navigating through Tides of Resource Optimization:
- A captain navigates through tides for efficiency. Leaders navigate through the "Tides of Resource Optimization," ensuring that resources are utilized effectively to maximize output.
- Regularly assess resource allocation and optimize workflows to eliminate inefficiencies. Navigate through the tides of resource optimization to ensure that the organization operates at its full potential. Similar to a captain navigating through tides, your leadership guides the organization through resource challenges with strategic efficiency.

The Lighthouse of Process Streamlining:
- A captain navigates by the light of a lighthouse. Leaders use the "Lighthouse of Process Streamlining" to illuminate the path toward streamlined and efficient processes.
- Evaluate and refine operational processes to eliminate bottlenecks and enhance efficiency. The lighthouse of process streamlining guides the organization through the challenges of complex operations, ensuring a clear and efficient path forward.
  Much like a captain navigating by a lighthouse, your leadership uses process streamlining as a guiding light for operational efficiency.

Harmonizing Team Efforts Like a Well-Tuned Crew:
- A captain harmonizes crew efforts for smooth operation. Leaders harmonize team efforts through effective communication, collaboration, and role alignment, ensuring that each member contributes to the organization's overall efficiency.
- Foster a collaborative environment, clarify roles and responsibilities, and encourage open communication to ensure that the team operates harmoniously. Much like a captain harmonizing crew efforts, your leadership aligns the team for optimal efficiency in achieving organizational goals.

The Sextant of Performance Metrics:
- A captain uses a sextant for navigation accuracy. Leaders use "The Sextant of Performance Metrics" to measure and assess operational effectiveness, guiding decisions based on accurate data.
- Implement performance metrics that provide insights into key operational areas.
  The sextant of performance metrics guides decision-making, helping the organization navigate through challenges with data-driven precision. Similar to a captain using a

sextant for accuracy, your leadership uses performance metrics for precise navigation of operational challenges.

Adjusting Sails for Market Agility:

- A captain adjusts sails for changing winds. Leaders adjust sails through "Market Agility," adapting operational strategies to align with evolving market conditions.
- Stay attuned to market trends and adjust operational strategies accordingly. The adjustment of sails for market agility ensures that the organization navigates through changing business landscapes with flexibility and responsiveness. Like a captain adjusting sails, your leadership adapts operational approaches to navigate market shifts successfully.

Maintaining standards and processes.

Leaders with the Captain Mariner Mindset recognize the crucial role of Maintaining Standards and Processes as essential navigation beacons. Similar to a captain ensuring the ship adheres to established standards, this analogical guide explores how well-crafted maintenance of standards and processes contributes to smooth sailing, creating positive waves within the organizational landscape.

The Ship's Logbook of Standards:

- A captain maintains a logbook of the ship's journey. Leaders keep a metaphorical "Ship's Logbook of Standards," documenting and upholding established norms and benchmarks.
- Establish clear standards for performance, conduct, and quality within the organization. Regularly update the Ship's Logbook to reflect evolving industry best practices and internal benchmarks. Like a captain's logbook, your leadership maintains standards that serve as a historical record of excellence and a guide for ongoing improvement.

The Anchors of Consistent Processes:

- A captain relies on anchors for stability. Leaders use the "Anchors of Consistent Processes" to provide stability and ensure that operations adhere to established workflows.
- Implement standardized processes for key operations, ensuring that every team member follows consistent workflows. The anchors of consistent processes stabilize operations, preventing deviations that could compromise efficiency. Similar to a captain relying on anchors, your leadership uses consistent processes to provide stability in day-to-day operations.

Charting a Course with Standard Operating Procedures:

- A captain charts a course for the ship. Leaders chart a course for the organization using "Standard Operating Procedures (SOPs)," ensuring that every aspect of the journey aligns with established protocols.
- Develop and regularly update SOPs for critical processes. Chart the organization's course by aligning actions with the established procedures, promoting efficiency and minimizing deviations. Much like a captain charting a course, your leadership uses SOPs to guide the organization towards its objectives with precision.

Navigating Storms with Compliance Measures:

- A captain navigates storms with precautionary measures. Leaders navigate organizational storms with "Compliance Measures," ensuring that every operation adheres to legal, ethical, and internal standards.
- Establish compliance measures to monitor adherence to standards and regulations. Navigate through organizational challenges by ensuring that all actions align with ethical guidelines and legal requirements. Like a captain navigating storms, your leadership guides the organization through challenges with a commitment to compliance.

Harmonizing the Crew with Standardization:
- A captain harmonizes the crew for seamless cooperation. Leaders harmonize the team through "Standardization," creating an environment where everyone understands and follows established norms.
- Foster a culture of standardization where team members are aligned with established processes and expectations. Harmonize the crew by ensuring that every member contributes to the collective efficiency through adherence to standards. Similar to a captain harmonizing the crew, your leadership standardizes processes for seamless cooperation.

Continuous improvement

Within the endless ocean of successful administration, pioneers with the Captain Sailor Mentality get it the noteworthiness of Nonstop Advancement as the wind that moves the dispatch toward brilliance. Comparative to a captain tirelessly looking for ideal courses, this analogical direct investigates how well-crafted ceaseless enhancement procedures contribute to smooth cruising, making positive waves inside the organizational scene.

The Navigator's Logbook of Insights:
- A captain maintains a logbook of navigational insights. Leaders keep a "Navigator's Logbook of Insights" in the form of a continuous improvement process, documenting lessons learned and strategies for refinement.
- Establish a systematic approach for gathering feedback, insights, and lessons from every operation. The Navigator's Logbook ensures that the organization learns from past experiences and consistently seeks ways to enhance performance. Much like a captain's logbook, your leadership cultivates a culture of learning and improvement.

Adjusting Sails with Feedback Winds:
- A captain adjusts the sails based on wind direction. Leaders adjust organizational strategies with the "Feedback Winds," ensuring that constructive feedback guides continuous improvement efforts.
- Encourage a culture where feedback is actively sought and valued. Adjust organizational strategies based on the winds of constructive feedback, leveraging insights to refine processes and operations. Similar to a captain adjusting sails, your leadership adapts strategies to navigate the evolving winds of improvement.

Navigating through Storms of Challenges:
- A captain navigates through storms with resilience. Leaders navigate through challenges using the "Storms of Challenges," turning obstacles into opportunities for improvement.
- Identify challenges as opportunities for growth and innovation. Navigating through storms of challenges allows the organization to strengthen its capabilities and enhance resilience. Like a captain navigating through storms, your leadership guides the organization through challenges with a focus on continuous improvement.

The Compass of Key Performance Indicators (KPIs):
- A captain uses a compass for direction. Leaders use the "Compass of Key Performance Indicators (KPIs)," providing a clear direction for improvement by tracking and analyzing essential metrics.
- Define and monitor KPIs that align with organizational goals. The Compass of KPIs guides the organization toward areas that require improvement, ensuring a focused and data-driven approach to continuous enhancement. Much like a captain using a compass, your leadership navigates through performance indicators for effective improvement.

Harvesting the Fruits of Innovation:

- A captain explores new territories for opportunities. Leaders explore new avenues through the "Harvesting of Innovation," encouraging creative solutions and groundbreaking ideas.
- Cultivate an environment that fosters innovation and creativity. Harvest the fruits of innovation by implementing novel approaches that contribute to organizational improvement. Similar to a captain exploring new territories, your leadership encourages the team to embrace innovation for continuous enhancement.

Chapter **14**

The Anchors of Ethics
Building an ethical workplace.

Within the tremendous ocean of viable administration, pioneers with the Captain Sailor Mentality recognize the foremost significance of Building an Moral Working environment as the compass that guides the transport towards maintainable victory. Comparable to a captain guaranteeing the team takes after moral standards, this analogical direct investigates how well-crafted methodologies for building an moral working environment contribute to smooth cruising, making positive waves inside the organizational scene.

The Moral Compass of Leadership:
- A captain uses a moral compass for navigation. Leaders employ the "Moral Compass of Leadership" to set a course of ethical behavior, guiding the organization with unwavering principles.
- Define and communicate a set of ethical values that serve as the moral compass for the organization. Uphold these principles in every decision and action, ensuring that ethical considerations guide the ship through calm and stormy seas alike.

Anchor of Trust in Crew Relationships:
- A captain relies on anchors for stability. Leaders establish an "Anchor of Trust" within the workplace, fostering stability through transparent and trustworthy relationships among team members.
- Cultivate an environment where trust is foundational to all interactions. The anchor of trust ensures that every member of the crew can rely on one another, promoting a workplace where ethical behavior is the bedrock of collaboration. Similar to a captain relying on anchors, your leadership fosters trust for stability in the workplace.

Sailing the Seas of Transparency:
- A captain sails through transparent waters for safe navigation. Leaders sail through the "Seas of Transparency," ensuring that openness and clarity characterize all organizational processes.
- Promote transparency in decision-making, communication, and operations. Navigating through transparent seas ensures that every action is visible, fostering an environment where ethical behavior is both expected and celebrated. Much like a captain sailing through transparent waters, your leadership guides the organization with openness and honesty.

Navigating Through Ethical Storms:
- A captain navigates through storms with caution. Leaders navigate through "Ethical Storms" with a proactive approach, addressing challenges to ethical principles before they escalate.
- Develop clear procedures for handling ethical dilemmas and misconduct. Navigating through ethical storms involves addressing issues promptly and implementing corrective measures to ensure the integrity of the workplace remains intact. Like a captain navigating through storms, your leadership guides the organization through challenges with ethical resilience.

The Guiding Stars of Ethical Leadership:
- A captain navigates by the stars. Leaders follow the "Guiding Stars of Ethical Leadership," embodying and exemplifying ethical behavior to inspire the entire crew.
- Lead by example, demonstrating ethical conduct in every aspect of leadership. The guiding stars of ethical leadership inspire others to follow suit, creating a workplace where ethical behavior is a shared commitment. Much like a captain navigating by the stars, your leadership serves as a beacon of ethical guidance.

Harboring a Culture of Accountability:
- A captain ensures accountability for every crew member. Leaders harbor a "Culture of Accountability," where individuals take responsibility for their actions, fostering an ethical workplace.
- Establish clear expectations for ethical behavior and hold everyone accountable for upholding these standards. The culture of accountability ensures that every member of the crew understands their role in maintaining an ethical workplace. Similar to a captain ensuring accountability, your leadership fosters a culture where ethical responsibility is shared by all.

Leading by example.
Leaders with the Captain Mariner Mindset understand the pivotal role of Leading by Example as the guiding light that steers the ship toward success. Similar to a captain setting the tone for the crew, this analogical guide explores how well-crafted strategies for leading by example contribute to smooth sailing, creating positive waves within the organizational landscape.

The Captain's Deck of Integrity:
- A captain's deck reflects unwavering integrity. Leaders maintain a metaphorical "Captain's Deck of Integrity," where every decision and action aligns with the highest ethical standards.
- Embody the values and principles you wish to see in your team. The Captain's Deck of Integrity ensures that your leadership sets a standard of honesty, fairness, and ethical behavior, inspiring others to follow suit. Much like a captain's deck reflecting integrity, your leadership becomes a beacon of ethical conduct.

The Compass of Consistency:
- A captain's compass guides with unwavering consistency.
  Leaders use the "Compass of Consistency" to ensure that their actions align with organizational values consistently.
- Model consistency in decision-making and behavior. The Compass of Consistency ensures that your leadership is a reliable guide for the team, promoting a stable and predictable work environment. Similar to a captain's consistent compass, your leadership provides a reliable direction for the team.

The Mast of Dedication and Hard Work:
- A captain's mast stands tall in dedication. Leaders erect the "Mast of Dedication and Hard Work," exemplifying a strong work ethic and commitment to excellence.
- Demonstrate a relentless dedication to your work. The Mast of Dedication and Hard Work sets the standard for a strong work ethic, motivating the team to invest their best efforts. Like a captain's mast standing tall, your leadership inspires dedication throughout the organization.

Navigating Storms with Calm Leadership:
- A captain navigates storms with calm authority. Leaders navigate through challenges with "Calm Leadership," maintaining composure and providing reassurance to the team.
- During turbulent times, exhibit calm and composed leadership. Navigating storms with Calm Leadership ensures that the team remains steady and focused even in challenging situations. Much like a captain navigating storms, your leadership guides the organization through difficulties with a steady hand.

The Signal Lantern of Team Collaboration:
- A captain signals through lanterns for team collaboration. Leaders use the "Signal Lantern of Team Collaboration," actively fostering a collaborative environment by being inclusive and approachable.
- Encourage open communication, collaboration, and approachability. The Signal Lantern of Team Collaboration sends a clear message that teamwork is essential,

inspiring a collaborative spirit within the organization. Similar to a captain signaling through lanterns, your leadership promotes a collaborative and inclusive workplace.

Handling ethical dilemmas.
Within the endless ocean of compelling administration, pioneers with the Captain Sailor Attitude recognize the unavoidable challenges of Taking care of Moral Situations as stormy waters that require cautious route. Comparative to a captain confronting ethical junction, this analogical direct investigates how well-crafted methodologies for taking care of moral problems contribute to smooth cruising, making positive waves inside the organizational scene.

The Navigator's Moral Map:
- A captain relies on a moral map for navigation. Leaders utilize a metaphorical "Navigator's Moral Map" to guide decisions during ethical dilemmas, ensuring a clear understanding of the ethical landscape.
- Establish a framework of ethical principles and values that acts as a moral map for the organization. The Navigator's Moral Map ensures that ethical decisions are aligned with the organization's values, offering guidance through complex dilemmas. Similar to a captain relying on a moral map, your leadership navigates through ethical challenges with a clear sense of direction.

Setting the Ethical Sail:
- A captain sets the sail for ethical navigation. Leaders engage in "Setting the Ethical Sail," proactively incorporating ethical considerations into the organizational culture and decision-making processes.
- Foster a culture that values ethical considerations in every aspect of operations. Setting the Ethical Sail ensures that ethical awareness becomes an integral part of decision-making, guiding the organization toward morally sound choices. Much like a captain setting the sail, your leadership directs the organization with an ethical course.

The Anchor of Ethical Consistency:
- A captain relies on anchors for stability. Leaders establish an "Anchor of Ethical Consistency," ensuring that ethical decisions are consistent with established principles and values.
- Uphold ethical consistency in decision-making, regardless of external pressures. The Anchor of Ethical Consistency stabilizes the organization by ensuring that ethical choices align with enduring values, fostering trust and credibility. Like a captain relying on anchors, your leadership maintains stability in ethical decision-making.

Navigating the Storms of Moral Ambiguity:
- A captain navigates through storms with caution. Leaders navigate through the "Storms of Moral Ambiguity" by approaching ethical dilemmas with careful consideration and thoughtful reflection.
- Develop a systematic approach for addressing moral ambiguity. Navigating the Storms of Moral Ambiguity involves seeking diverse perspectives, consulting ethical guidelines, and making decisions with a profound understanding of potential consequences. Similar to a captain navigating through storms, your leadership addresses moral ambiguity with resilience.

The Lighthouse of Ethical Guidance:
- A captain navigates by the light of a lighthouse. Leaders use the "Lighthouse of Ethical Guidance" to illuminate the path through ethical dilemmas, providing a beacon for the organization to follow.
- Establish channels for seeking ethical guidance, whether through a dedicated ethics committee, ethical mentors, or regular ethical training. The Lighthouse of Ethical Guidance ensures that the organization remains on course during ethical dilemmas, guided by the principles of integrity.

Chapter 15

Treasure Map: Incentives and Rewards
Designing effective incentive programs.

Similar to a captain steering towards favorable winds, this analogical guide explores how well-crafted strategies for designing effective incentive programs contribute to smooth sailing, creating positive waves within the organizational landscape.

The Sails of Recognition and Rewards:
- A captain adjusts the sails for optimal wind capture. Leaders adjust the "Sails of Recognition and Rewards," ensuring that incentive programs capture the favorable winds of employee motivation.
- Tailor recognition and rewards to align with individual and team achievements. The Sails of Recognition and Rewards maximize the potential for motivating the crew, harnessing the power of positive reinforcement for sustained effort. Similar to a captain adjusting sails for optimal wind, your leadership customizes incentives to inspire the team effectively.

Navigating with a North Star of Performance Metrics:
- A captain navigates using the North Star for direction. Leaders use a "North Star of Performance Metrics" to guide the design of incentive programs, aligning them with organizational goals.
- Define clear performance metrics that lead towards organizational success. The North Star of Performance Metrics ensures that incentive programs are not only motivating but also directed towards achieving key objectives. Like a captain navigating with the North Star, your leadership uses performance metrics as a guiding light for incentive design.

The Compass of Fairness and Equality:
- A captain uses a compass for accurate navigation. Leaders use the "Compass of Fairness and Equality" to guide the distribution of incentives, ensuring they are perceived as just and equitable.
- Design incentive programs that are transparent and fair. The Compass of Fairness and Equality ensures that incentives are distributed objectively, promoting a sense of justice and equality among the crew. Much like a captain using a compass, your leadership ensures fair navigation in the incentive program design.

Setting a Course with Individualized Goals:
- A captain plots a course based on the ship's capabilities. Leaders set a course with "Individualized Goals," tailoring incentive programs to individual strengths and aspirations.
- Recognize and accommodate diverse talents and motivations within the team. Setting a Course with Individualized Goals ensures that incentive programs are personally relevant, motivating each team member to strive for their unique potential. Similar to a captain plotting a course, your leadership tailors incentives to accommodate individual capabilities.

The Harbor of Team Collaboration Bonuses:
- A captain rewards the crew for collective efforts. Leaders establish a "Harbor of Team Collaboration Bonuses," recognizing and rewarding group achievements that contribute to smooth sailing.
- Encourage collaboration and teamwork through collective incentives. The Harbor of Team Collaboration Bonuses ensures that collective efforts are celebrated, fostering a culture of collaboration among the crew. Like a captain rewarding the crew, your leadership acknowledges and rewards teamwork in the incentive program.

Navigating Storms with Resilience Bonuses:
- A captain provides bonuses for navigating storms with resilience. Leaders offer "Navigating Storms with Resilience Bonuses," recognizing and rewarding employees who face challenges with perseverance and resilience.
- Acknowledge and reward resilience during challenging times. Navigating Storms with Resilience Bonuses ensures that employees are motivated to overcome obstacles, contributing to the overall resilience of the organization. Much like a captain providing bonuses for resilience, your leadership recognizes and rewards resilience in the face of adversity.

The psychology of rewards.

Comparative to a captain understanding the streams for ideal route, this analogical direct investigates how well-crafted techniques for comprehending the brain research of rewards contribute to smooth cruising, making positive waves inside the organizational scene.

The Tides of Intrinsic and Extrinsic Motivation:
- A captain navigates the tides for optimal course setting. Leaders understand the "Tides of Intrinsic and Extrinsic Motivation," recognizing that effective rewards encompass both internal and external sources of motivation.
- Balance intrinsic rewards like personal growth and job satisfaction with extrinsic rewards such as bonuses or recognition. The Tides of Intrinsic and Extrinsic Motivation ensure that the crew is motivated from within and by external factors, creating a well-rounded and sustainable motivational environment. Much like a captain navigating tides, your leadership leverages both intrinsic and extrinsic motivators for optimal results.

The Winds of Timing and Frequency:
- A captain adjusts sails to harness favorable winds. Leaders harness the "Winds of Timing and Frequency," understanding that the timing and frequency of rewards significantly impact their motivational effectiveness.
- Consider when and how often rewards are provided. The Winds of Timing and Frequency ensure that rewards are timely and consistent, maximizing their impact on employee motivation. Similar to a captain adjusting sails for optimal winds, your leadership fine-tunes the timing and frequency of rewards.

The Trade Winds of Personalization:
- A captain navigates through personalized trade winds. Leaders harness the "Trade Winds of Personalization," recognizing that personalized rewards resonate more deeply with individuals.
- Tailor rewards to individual preferences and aspirations. The Trade Winds of Personalization ensure that rewards are meaningful and relevant to each team member, fostering a sense of appreciation and motivation. Like a captain navigating through personalized trade winds, your leadership personalizes rewards for maximum impact.

The Ripples of Immediate Recognition:
- A captain acknowledges favorable ripples in the water. Leaders create "Ripples of Immediate Recognition," understanding that timely acknowledgment enhances the impact of rewards.
- Recognize achievements promptly and consistently. The Ripples of Immediate Recognition ensure that employees receive timely acknowledgment for their efforts, creating a positive and motivating work environment. Much like a captain acknowledging ripples, your leadership ensures immediate recognition for noteworthy achievements.

The Depths of Value Perception:
- A captain navigates through varying sea depths. Leaders fathom the "Depths of Value Perception," recognizing that the perceived value of rewards differs among individuals.
- Understand the unique values and preferences of your team members. The Depths of Value Perception ensure that rewards are perceived as valuable, aligning with the diverse motivations within the team. Similar to a captain navigating through varying sea depths, your leadership considers individual perceptions for effective reward strategies.

Personalizing incentives to improve performance.
Similar to a captain adjusting the helm for optimal navigation, this analogical guide explores how well-crafted strategies for personalizing incentives contribute to smooth sailing, creating positive waves within the organizational landscape.

Navigating the Waters of Individual Aspirations:
- A captain plots a course based on individual crew skills. Leaders navigate the "Waters of Individual Aspirations," recognizing that personalized incentives are crafted based on the unique aspirations and skills of each team member.
- Understand the individual goals and aspirations of your team members. Navigating the Waters of Individual Aspirations ensures that incentives are aligned with personal motivations, motivating each member to contribute their best. Similar to a captain plotting a course based on crew skills, your leadership tailors incentives to individual aspirations.

The Compass of Personal Recognition:
- A captain adjusts the compass for precise navigation. Leaders use the "Compass of Personal Recognition" to navigate the intricate landscape of individual contributions, ensuring that personalized recognition plays a pivotal role in the incentive program.
- Acknowledge and celebrate individual achievements in a personalized manner. The Compass of Personal Recognition ensures that each team member feels seen and appreciated, motivating them to excel in their unique roles. Like a captain adjusting the compass for precise navigation, your leadership employs personalized recognition for individual contributions.

Setting Sail with Tailored Goals:
- A captain sets sail with a course tailored to the ship's capabilities. Leaders set sail with "Tailored Goals," customizing performance objectives to align with each team member's skills and developmental areas.
- Establish goals that challenge and resonate with individual capabilities. Setting Sail with Tailored Goals ensures that team members are motivated by goals that are personally meaningful, contributing to improved performance.
  Similar to a captain setting a course tailored to the ship's capabilities, your leadership tailors goals to individual skills.

Harvesting the Winds of Individual Preferences:
- A captain adjusts sails to harness personalized winds. Leaders harvest the "Winds of Individual Preferences," recognizing that incentive preferences vary among team members.
- Understand and accommodate individual preferences in incentive structures. Harvesting the Winds of Individual Preferences ensures that the incentive program resonates with each team member, optimizing motivation. Like a captain adjusting sails to harness personalized winds, your leadership tailors incentives to individual preferences.

Chapter **16**

Captain's Log: Documenting the Journey
The necessity of keeping records.

In the vast sea of effective management, leaders with the Captain Mariner Mindset understand the indispensable role of Keeping Records as the logbook that chronicles the journey and lessons learned. Similar to a captain maintaining a ship's log for navigation, this analogical guide explores how conscientious record-keeping contributes to smooth sailing, creating positive waves within the organizational landscape.

The Ship's Log of Achievements and Milestones:
- A captain diligently records the ship's achievements and milestones. Leaders maintain the "Ship's Log of Achievements and Milestones," chronicling significant successes and milestones within the organization.
- Document and celebrate noteworthy accomplishments. The Ship's Log of Achievements and Milestones ensures a historical record that inspires the crew and provides a guide for future endeavors. Much like a captain maintaining a log of achievements, your leadership keeps a record of significant organizational milestones.

Navigating the Winds of Decision-Making:
- A captain logs decisions made during the journey. Leaders navigate the "Winds of Decision-Making" by recording significant decisions, their context, and outcomes.
- Keep a decision log to track the rationale behind choices. Navigating the Winds of Decision-Making ensures a transparent record, fostering accountability and providing valuable insights for future choices. Similar to a captain logging decisions, your leadership maintains a record of key organizational choices.

The Lighthouse of Lessons Learned:
- A captain notes lessons learned from navigating tricky waters. Leaders establish the "Lighthouse of Lessons Learned," documenting insights gained from both successes and challenges.
- Record and analyze lessons learned from various experiences. The Lighthouse of Lessons Learned ensures that the organization benefits from past wisdom, minimizing the risk of repeating mistakes and maximizing opportunities for growth. Like a captain noting lessons from tricky waters, your leadership maintains a record of valuable insights.

The Navigator's Journal of Team Performance:
- A captain keeps a journal of crew performance. Leaders maintain the "Navigator's Journal of Team Performance," documenting individual and collective achievements, challenges, and improvements.
- Regularly update records on team dynamics and performance. The Navigator's Journal of Team Performance serves as a reference for identifying patterns, acknowledging achievements, and addressing areas for development. Much like a captain keeping a journal of crew performance, your leadership tracks and evaluates team dynamics.

Charting the Course of Employee Development:
- A captain records the career progression of crew members. Leaders embark on "Charting the Course of Employee Development," documenting individual growth, skills acquired, and career milestones.
- Maintain records of employee development and achievements. Charting the Course of Employee Development helps identify potential leaders, tailor training programs, and foster a culture of continuous improvement. Similar to a captain recording crew career progression, your leadership tracks individual and team development.

The Ledger of Organizational Culture:
- A captain keeps a ledger of the ship's culture. Leaders maintain the "Ledger of Organizational Culture," documenting cultural values, rituals, and noteworthy cultural moments.
- Record elements that define and shape the organization's culture. The Ledger of Organizational Culture ensures continuity in cultural practices and helps align new initiatives with established values. Like a captain keeping a ledger of ship culture, your leadership records and preserves the essence of the organizational culture.

Utilizing data for better management decisions.

Leaders with the Captain Mariner Mindset recognize the transformative power of Utilizing Data as the compass that guides decision-making and ensures a course toward organizational success. Similar to a captain relying on navigational instruments, this analogical guide explores how adeptly utilizing data contributes to smooth sailing, creating positive waves within the organizational landscape.

The Sextant of Strategic Insight:
- A captain uses a sextant to determine position and plan the course. Leaders wield the "Sextant of Strategic Insight," utilizing data to understand the current organizational position and plan strategic courses for the future.
- Leverage data to gain insights into market trends, customer preferences, and internal performance. The Sextant of Strategic Insight ensures informed decision-making, allowing the organization to navigate towards success with a clear understanding of its position. Much like a captain using a sextant for navigation, your leadership employs data for strategic planning.

Charting the Seas of Employee Productivity:
- A captain monitors ship systems for optimal performance. Leaders embark on "Charting the Seas of Employee Productivity," using data to track and enhance workforce efficiency and engagement.
- Utilize data analytics to measure employee performance, identify strengths, and address areas for improvement. Charting the Seas of Employee Productivity ensures that resources are allocated effectively, fostering a culture of high-performance. Similar to a captain monitoring ship systems, your leadership uses data to optimize workforce productivity.

The Compass of Customer Insights:
- A captain relies on a compass for direction. Leaders follow the "Compass of Customer Insights," utilizing data to understand customer needs, behaviors, and preferences.
- Leverage customer data to tailor products and services. The Compass of Customer Insights ensures that decision-making aligns with customer expectations, creating a customer-centric approach. Like a captain relying on a compass, your leadership uses customer data to guide strategic decisions.

The Weather Vane of Market Trends:
- A captain observes the weather vane for changing winds. Leaders watch the "Weather Vane of Market Trends," using data to stay attuned to shifts in the business environment.
- Monitor market trends and adapt strategies accordingly. The Weather Vane of Market Trends ensures that the organization remains agile, ready to navigate changing industry landscapes. Much like a captain observing a weather vane, your leadership uses data to stay informed about market dynamics.

The Barometer of Financial Performance:
- A captain monitors the barometer for atmospheric pressure changes. Leaders utilize the "Barometer of Financial Performance," using data to assess the financial health of the organization.

- Analyze financial data to make informed decisions about investments, budgeting, and resource allocation. The Barometer of Financial Performance ensures that the organization sails with financial stability and resilience. Similar to a captain monitoring a barometer, your leadership relies on financial data for sound decision-making.

Legal compliance and documentation.
Similar to a captain meticulously adhering to maritime laws, this analogical guide explores how conscientious legal compliance and documentation contribute to smooth sailing, creating positive waves within the organizational landscape.

The Legal Compass of Maritime Regulations:
- A captain relies on a legal compass for navigation. Leaders use the "Legal Compass of Maritime Regulations," ensuring that the organization adheres to applicable laws and regulations.
- Stay informed about industry-specific laws and regulations. The Legal Compass of Maritime Regulations ensures that your organization navigates the legal landscape with precision, minimizing the risk of legal complications. Like a captain relying on a legal compass, your leadership guides the organization in alignment with applicable regulations.

Documenting the Ship's Manifest of Policies:
- A captain maintains a ship's manifest detailing cargo and equipment. Leaders create the "Ship's Manifest of Policies," documenting the organization's policies, procedures, and guidelines.
- Develop, update, and communicate policies to ensure a clear understanding across the organization. Documenting the Ship's Manifest of Policies provides a foundation for legal compliance and helps in establishing a culture of transparency. Similar to a captain maintaining a ship's manifest, your leadership keeps a record of organizational policies.

The Navigational Charts of Employment Law:
- A captain studies navigational charts for safe passage. Leaders consult the "Navigational Charts of Employment Law," understanding and adhering to labor laws and regulations.
- Keep abreast of employment laws to ensure fair and legal practices. The Navigational Charts of Employment Law serve as a guide, helping your leadership make informed decisions in areas such as hiring, termination, and employee relations. Like a captain studying navigational charts, your leadership navigates employment laws for a smooth journey.

Maintaining the Captain's Log of Employee Records:
- A captain maintains a log detailing crew activities.
  Leaders keep the "Captain's Log of Employee Records," recording essential employee information, performance, and disciplinary actions.
- Document employee records systematically and securely. Maintaining the Captain's Log of Employee Records ensures compliance with privacy laws and facilitates fair treatment of employees. Much like a captain keeping a log of crew activities, your leadership maintains a secure record of employee-related information.

The Safety Inspection Checklist of Workplace Conditions:
- A captain inspects the ship for safety compliance. Leaders use the "Safety Inspection Checklist of Workplace Conditions," ensuring that the working environment complies with health and safety regulations.
- : Regularly inspect and address workplace safety concerns. The Safety Inspection Checklist of Workplace Conditions ensures legal compliance, safeguarding the well-

being of employees. Similar to a captain inspecting the ship, your leadership conducts regular safety checks in the workplace.

Chapter **17**

Managing Multicultural Crews
Appreciating diversity.

Within the tremendous ocean of successful administration, pioneers with the Captain Sailor Mentality recognize the transformative control of Increasing in value Differences as the wind that fills the sails of development and collaboration. Comparable to a captain grasping differing winds for ideal route, this analogical direct investigates how cultivating a culture of differing qualities contributes to smooth cruising, making positive waves inside the organizational scene.

Navigating the Tides of Diverse Perspectives:
- A captain adjusts the course based on changing tides. Leaders navigate the "Tides of Diverse Perspectives," understanding that a diverse team brings unique viewpoints, enriching the organization's journey.
- Encourage open communication and actively seek input from diverse team members. Navigating the Tides of Diverse Perspectives ensures a rich pool of ideas and solutions, enhancing decision-making. Much like a captain adjusting the course with changing tides, your leadership adapts to the diversity of perspectives within the team.

The Crew Mosaic of Unique Talents:
- A captain values each crew member's unique skills. Leaders appreciate the "Crew Mosaic of Unique Talents," recognizing that diversity extends beyond demographics to include varied talents and strengths.
- Acknowledge and leverage the diverse skills of team members. The Crew Mosaic of Unique Talents ensures that each individual contributes their strengths, fostering a collaborative and high-performing team. Similar to a captain valuing each crew member's skills, your leadership appreciates the unique talents within the team.

Harvesting the Winds of Cultural Richness:
- A captain harnesses winds from diverse cultures. Leaders harvest the "Winds of Cultural Richness," appreciating the cultural diversity within the team.
- Embrace cultural differences and promote a culturally inclusive environment. Harvesting the Winds of Cultural Richness ensures that diverse backgrounds contribute to a vibrant organizational culture, fostering creativity and adaptability. Like a captain harnessing winds from diverse cultures, your leadership embraces and celebrates cultural richness.

The Lighthouse of Inclusive Leadership:
- A captain's lighthouse guides safely through diverse waters. Leaders become the "Lighthouse of Inclusive Leadership," providing guidance and creating a safe environment where diverse voices are heard and valued.
- Foster a culture of inclusion through leadership practices that promote diversity. The Lighthouse of Inclusive Leadership ensures that team members feel respected, included, and empowered to contribute their best. Much like a captain's lighthouse guiding through diverse waters, your leadership illuminates the path of inclusive practices.

Navigating the Currents of Diverse Experiences:
- A captain navigates through currents of varying strengths. Leaders navigate the "Currents of Diverse Experiences," recognizing that individuals bring unique professional backgrounds and experiences.
- Leverage the richness of diverse experiences to enhance problem-solving and innovation. Navigating the Currents of Diverse Experiences ensures that the team benefits from a broad range of perspectives, contributing to organizational success.

Similar to a captain navigating through diverse currents, your leadership steers through the varying strengths of individual experiences.

The Bridge of Inclusive Communication:
- A captain ensures clear communication across the ship. Leaders build the "Bridge of Inclusive Communication," fostering an environment where all team members feel heard and understood.
- Establish open channels for communication and actively listen to diverse voices. The Bridge of Inclusive Communication ensures that information flows seamlessly, promoting collaboration and cohesion. Like a captain ensuring clear communication across the ship, your leadership builds bridges for inclusive communication.

Overcoming cultural barriers.

Leaders with the Captain understand the importance of Overcoming Cultural Barriers as the compass that guides the ship through diverse waters. Similar to a captain steering through varied cultures for seamless navigation, this analogical guide explores how adeptly addressing cultural barriers contributes to smooth sailing, creating positive waves within the organizational landscape.

The Compass of Cultural Understanding:
- A captain relies on a compass to navigate. Leaders use the "Compass of Cultural Understanding," recognizing that understanding diverse cultures is essential for effective leadership.
- Invest time in learning about different cultural norms, customs, and communication styles. The Compass of Cultural Understanding ensures that leaders can navigate through diverse teams with cultural sensitivity, fostering mutual respect. Similar to a captain relying on a compass, your leadership utilizes cultural understanding as a guide.

Building Bridges Across Cultural Channels:
- A captain builds bridges for safe passage. Leaders construct the "Bridges Across Cultural Channels," establishing communication channels that connect team members from different cultural backgrounds.
- Facilitate open and inclusive communication to bridge cultural gaps. Building Bridges Across Cultural Channels ensures that team members feel heard and understood, promoting collaboration and reducing misunderstandings. Like a captain building bridges for safe passage, your leadership constructs channels for effective cross-cultural communication.

The Multilingual Deck of Inclusive Communication:
- A captain ensures effective communication on a multilingual deck. Leaders maintain the "Multilingual Deck of Inclusive Communication," fostering an environment where language differences are considered and accommodated.
- Promote language inclusivity and provide tools for effective communication. The Multilingual Deck of Inclusive Communication ensures that language barriers don't hinder collaboration, creating a harmonious and inclusive workplace.
  Similar to a captain ensuring effective communication on a multilingual deck, your leadership promotes language inclusivity.

Navigating the Shoals of Cultural Sensitivity:
- A captain navigates through treacherous shoals. Leaders navigate the "Shoals of Cultural Sensitivity," understanding potential pitfalls and challenges that may arise due to cultural differences.
- Foster cultural sensitivity within the team and address potential cultural conflicts proactively. Navigating the Shoals of Cultural Sensitivity ensures a harmonious work environment, where diverse perspectives are valued and respected. Like a captain navigating through treacherous shoals, your leadership steers through potential cultural challenges.

Fostering an inclusive environment.

Similar to a captain ensuring every crew member feels welcome on board, this analogical guide explores how fostering an inclusive environment contributes to smooth sailing, creating positive waves within the organizational landscape.

The Compass of Inclusive Leadership:
- A captain uses a compass for guidance. Leaders wield the "Compass of Inclusive Leadership," ensuring that their actions and decisions align with fostering an inclusive environment.
- Lead by example, demonstrating behaviors that promote inclusivity. The Compass of Inclusive Leadership guides the organization toward an environment where diversity is celebrated and all voices are heard. Much like a captain relying on a compass, your leadership follows the direction set by the principles of inclusive leadership.

Cultivating the Soil of Equal Opportunity:
- A captain ensures the ship's soil is fertile for growth. Leaders cultivate the "Soil of Equal Opportunity," creating conditions where every team member has a fair chance to grow and thrive.
- Implement policies and practices that ensure equal opportunities for professional growth. Cultivating the Soil of Equal Opportunity ensures that each individual, regardless of background, has the chance to flourish within the organization. Like a captain ensuring fertile soil, your leadership creates an environment where equal opportunities abound.

The Inclusive Harbor of Respectful Communication:
- A captain maintains clear communication within the harbor. Leaders establish the "Inclusive Harbor of Respectful Communication," fostering an environment where team members communicate respectfully, acknowledging diverse perspectives.
- Promote open, transparent, and respectful communication. The Inclusive Harbor of Respectful Communication ensures that every team member feels comfortable expressing their thoughts and ideas.

The Garden of Diverse Perspectives:
- A captain appreciates the diverse flora on an island. Leaders tend to the "Garden of Diverse Perspectives," recognizing that each unique viewpoint is a valuable contribution to the organizational landscape.
- Encourage the sharing of diverse opinions and perspectives. The Garden of Diverse Perspectives ensures that the organization benefits from a rich array of ideas, enhancing problem-solving and innovation. Like a captain appreciating the diverse flora, your leadership values and nourishes diverse perspectives.

Harmony in the Crew Symphony:
- A captain orchestrates a harmonious symphony among the crew. Leaders create "Harmony in the Crew Symphony," fostering an environment where every team member contributes to the collective success in a unified manner.
- Build a cohesive team where individuals complement each other's strengths. Harmony in the Crew Symphony ensures that diverse talents blend seamlessly, resulting in a high-performing and collaborative team. Much like a captain orchestrating a harmonious symphony, your leadership ensures unity among diverse talents.

Chapter **18**

The Open Seas: Dealing with Competition
Analyzing competitors.

Mariner Mindset recognize the importance of Analyzing Competitors as the strategic navigation tool that helps the ship chart its course amidst competitive waters. Similar to a captain studying the tactics of rival ships, this analogical guide explores how adeptly analyzing competitors contributes to smooth sailing, creating positive waves within the organizational landscape.

The Spyglass of Market Surveillance:
- A captain uses a spyglass to observe distant ships. Leaders wield the "Spyglass of Market Surveillance," constantly scanning the horizon for competitor movements and industry trends.
- Implement mechanisms for real-time market monitoring and competitor analysis. The Spyglass of Market Surveillance ensures that your leadership is informed about industry shifts, allowing the organization to adapt strategies accordingly. Much like a captain using a spyglass, your leadership observes and stays aware of competitor activities.

Charting the Competitor Map:
- A captain charts maps to navigate unfamiliar territories. Leaders engage in "Charting the Competitor Map," creating visual representations of competitor landscapes to inform strategic decision-making.
- Develop competitor maps that outline key players, strengths, weaknesses, and market positions. Charting the Competitor Map provides a comprehensive view of the competitive environment, aiding in strategic planning. Similar to a captain charting maps for navigation, your leadership maps out the competitive terrain.

The Trade Winds of Competitive Intelligence:
- A captain relies on trade winds for favorable sailing conditions. Leaders leverage the "Trade Winds of Competitive Intelligence," utilizing data and insights to gain a competitive advantage.
- Establish robust processes for gathering and analyzing competitive intelligence. The Trade Winds of Competitive Intelligence propel the organization forward by identifying opportunities and potential challenges. Like a captain harnessing trade winds, your leadership maximizes favorable conditions through strategic insights.

Navigating Through the Storms of Competitive Threats:
- A captain navigates through stormy weather. Leaders navigate the "Storms of Competitive Threats," understanding and preparing for challenges posed by aggressive competitors.
- Conduct risk assessments to identify potential competitive threats and develop contingency plans. Navigating Through the Storms of Competitive Threats ensures the organization can weather competitive challenges successfully. Much like a captain navigating through stormy weather, your leadership anticipates and mitigates competitive threats.

The Lighthouse of Market Positioning:
- A captain relies on a lighthouse for safe navigation. Leaders establish the "Lighthouse of Market Positioning," strategically positioning the organization to stand out amidst competitors.
- Develop a unique value proposition and communicate it clearly to stakeholders. The Lighthouse of Market Positioning guides the organization to a distinct and favorable

position in the market. Similar to a captain relying on a lighthouse, your leadership ensures a clear and visible market positioning.

The Pirate's Telescope of Competitive Benchmarking:

- A captain uses a telescope to benchmark rivals' strategies. Leaders adopt the "Pirate's Telescope of Competitive Benchmarking," comparing organizational performance and strategies against industry benchmarks.
- Regularly benchmark key performance indicators against industry standards. The Pirate's Telescope of Competitive Benchmarking provides insights for continuous improvement and innovation. Like a captain using a telescope to observe rivals, your leadership monitors and benchmarks against industry standards.

Developing a competitive edge.

Similar to a captain ensuring their cutlass is sharp for swift navigation, this analogical guide explores how adeptly developing a competitive edge contributes to smooth sailing, creating positive waves within the organizational landscape.

The Smithy of Innovation and Creativity:

- A captain relies on skilled smiths to craft a sharp cutlass. Leaders utilize the "Smithy of Innovation and Creativity," fostering an environment where inventive ideas are forged to gain a competitive edge.
- Encourage a culture of innovation and provide resources for creative thinking. The Smithy of Innovation and Creativity ensures that the organization sharpens its competitive cutlass through continuous ideation and improvement. Much like a captain relying on skilled smiths, your leadership cultivates a culture of innovation.

Navigating the Trade Routes of Market Trends:

- A captain navigates well-known trade routes for strategic advantage.
Leaders navigate the "Trade Routes of Market Trends," identifying and capitalizing on emerging trends for a competitive edge.
- Stay vigilant about market trends and adapt strategies accordingly. Navigating the Trade Routes of Market Trends allows the organization to position itself advantageously in response to changing market dynamics. Like a captain navigating trade routes, your leadership exploits market trends for strategic advantage.

The Mariner's Compass of Customer Insights:

- A captain uses a compass to find the best route. Leaders leverage the "Mariner's Compass of Customer Insights," understanding customer needs and preferences to guide strategic decision-making.
- Invest in customer research and feedback mechanisms. The Mariner's Compass of Customer Insights ensures that the organization steers its strategies towards customer satisfaction, gaining a competitive edge. Similar to a captain using a compass, your leadership relies on customer insights for effective navigation.

The Crow's Nest of Strategic Vision:

- A captain's crow's nest provides a high vantage point.
Leaders establish the "Crow's Nest of Strategic Vision," maintaining a high-level view to anticipate industry shifts and plan for the future.
- Foster a long-term strategic vision and set ambitious goals. The Crow's Nest of Strategic Vision ensures that the organization is prepared for upcoming challenges and seizes opportunities for a sustained competitive edge. Much like a captain using a crow's nest, your leadership maintains foresight for effective strategic planning.

The Armory of Talent Development:

- A captain ensures the crew is skilled with weapons. Leaders maintain the "Armory of Talent Development," investing in the continuous growth and development of the team to enhance organizational capabilities.

- Prioritize employee training, mentorship, and skill-building programs. The Armory of Talent Development ensures that the organization's workforce remains sharp and adaptable, contributing to a sustainable competitive edge. Like a captain maintaining an armory, your leadership invests in the continuous improvement of organizational talent.

Ethical competition.

Mariner Mindset recognize the moral compass of Ethical Competition as the guiding star that ensures the ship navigates the waters with integrity and honor. Similar to a captain steering by ethical principles, this analogical guide explores how adeptly embracing ethical competition contributes to smooth sailing, creating positive waves within the organizational landscape.

The Compass of Integrity:
- A captain relies on a compass for accurate navigation. Leaders wield the "Compass of Integrity," ensuring that decisions and actions align with ethical principles for true and honorable navigation.
- Establish and communicate clear ethical guidelines. The Compass of Integrity ensures that the organization sails true north, maintaining a reputation for honesty and transparency. Much like a captain relying on a compass, your leadership navigates with unwavering integrity.

Navigating the Fair Winds of Transparency:
- A captain sails in fair winds for smooth navigation.
  Leaders navigate the "Fair Winds of Transparency," fostering a culture where openness and honesty prevail, providing a clear view of the ethical path ahead.
- Communicate openly with stakeholders and employees. Navigating the Fair Winds of Transparency ensures that the organization operates with clarity, building trust and credibility. Like a captain sailing in fair winds, your leadership promotes a transparent and ethical workplace.

The North Star of Ethical Leadership:
- A captain uses the North Star for guidance. Leaders follow the "North Star of Ethical Leadership," setting an unwavering example of ethical behavior to guide the entire team.
- Demonstrate ethical behavior in all aspects of leadership. The North Star of Ethical Leadership ensures that the organization's moral compass is aligned, inspiring others to uphold ethical standards. Similar to a captain using the North Star, your leadership provides a constant guide for ethical decision-making.

Charting the Ethical Course:
- A captain charts a course for a safe journey. Leaders engage in "Charting the Ethical Course," mapping out strategies and plans that prioritize ethical considerations.
- Incorporate ethics into strategic decision-making. Charting the Ethical Course ensures that the organization stays on a path of integrity, avoiding ethical pitfalls. Much like a captain charting a safe journey, your leadership plans with ethics at the forefront.

Harboring in the Port of Fair Play:
- A captain harbors in a safe port for respite. Leaders anchor in the "Port of Fair Play," promoting an ethical culture where competition is driven by fairness and respect.
- Encourage fair competition and discourage unethical practices. Harboring in the Port of Fair Play ensures that the organization's success is built on merit and fair business practices. Like a captain finding respite in a safe port, your leadership fosters an environment of ethical competition.

Chapter **19**

Navigating Regulations and Compliance
Understanding industry laws and regulations.

In the vast sea of effective management, leaders with the Captain Mariner Mindset recognize the importance of Navigating Legal Waters as the sextant that ensures the ship sails within the boundaries of industry laws and regulations. Similar to a captain understanding maritime laws, this analogical guide explores how adeptly understanding industry laws and regulations contributes to smooth sailing, creating positive waves within the organizational landscape.

The Sextant of Legal Navigation:
- A captain uses a sextant for accurate navigation. Leaders wield the "Sextant of Legal Navigation," ensuring that organizational decisions and actions are aligned with industry laws and regulations for precise and lawful navigation.
- Establish a legal compliance framework and stay informed about industry regulations. The Sextant of Legal Navigation ensures that the organization sails within legal boundaries, avoiding potential legal storms.
  Similar to a captain using a sextant, your leadership navigates with a clear understanding of legal considerations.

Navigating the Currents of Compliance:
- A captain navigates ocean currents for efficient travel. Leaders navigate the "Currents of Compliance," continuously monitoring and adapting strategies to meet evolving legal requirements for efficient and compliant operations.
- Implement robust compliance mechanisms and stay abreast of legal updates. Navigating the Currents of Compliance ensures that the organization sails smoothly through changing legal landscapes. Much like a captain navigating ocean currents, your leadership adapts to legal currents for seamless compliance.

The Legal Lighthouse of Regulatory Awareness:
- A captain relies on a lighthouse for safe navigation. Leaders establish the "Legal Lighthouse of Regulatory Awareness," maintaining a vigilant lookout for changes in industry regulations that could impact the organization's course.
- Regularly review and update the organization's understanding of industry laws and regulations.
- The Legal Lighthouse of Regulatory Awareness ensures that the organization remains aware and prepared for any legal changes. Like a captain relying on a lighthouse, your leadership provides a clear view of legal considerations.

Setting Sail with Ethical Compliance:
- A captain ensures the crew adheres to ethical guidelines. Leaders set sail with "Ethical Compliance," fostering a culture where legal and ethical considerations are embedded in every aspect of organizational operations.
- Integrate ethical considerations into legal compliance practices. Setting Sail with Ethical Compliance ensures that the organization operates within legal boundaries while maintaining ethical standards. Similar to a captain ensuring ethical behavior, your leadership upholds both legal and ethical compliance.

The Legal Crew Manifest:
- A captain keeps a crew manifest for accountability. Leaders maintain the "Legal Crew Manifest," a comprehensive record of legal and regulatory compliance efforts, ensuring accountability and transparency.
- Develop and maintain detailed records of compliance efforts. The Legal Crew Manifest ensures that the organization can demonstrate its commitment to legal

compliance, fostering trust with stakeholders. Much like a captain keeping a crew manifest, your leadership maintains a transparent record of legal compliance.

Harboring in the Port of Due Diligence:
- A captain harbors in a safe port for thorough inspection. Leaders anchor in the "Port of Due Diligence," conducting regular audits and assessments to ensure all legal requirements are met.
- Establish a robust due diligence process to assess legal compliance. Harboring in the Port of Due Diligence ensures that the organization is continually refining its understanding and adherence to industry laws and regulations. Like a captain inspecting a safe port, your leadership conducts thorough assessments of legal compliance.

Implementing compliance strategies.

Similar to a captain charting a course for compliance, this analogical guide explores how adeptly implementing compliance strategies contributes to smooth sailing, creating positive waves within the organizational landscape.

The Navigation Chart of Compliance:
- A captain relies on a navigation chart for route planning. Leaders utilize the "Navigation Chart of Compliance," mapping out a comprehensive strategy that outlines the steps and considerations required for adherence to legal and regulatory requirements.
- Develop a detailed compliance strategy that encompasses all relevant regulations and standards. The Navigation Chart of Compliance serves as the roadmap for the organization, ensuring that it sails through regulatory waters with precision. Much like a captain relying on a navigation chart, your leadership plans for compliance with a clear strategy.

Setting Sail with Regulatory Awareness:
- A captain stays aware of sea conditions for safe navigation.
  Leaders set sail with "Regulatory Awareness," fostering a culture within the organization that prioritizes staying informed about the ever-changing legal and regulatory landscape.
- Implement mechanisms for continuous monitoring of regulatory changes. Setting Sail with Regulatory Awareness ensures that the organization remains agile, adapting strategies to comply with new regulations. Similar to a captain staying aware of sea conditions, your leadership stays vigilant about regulatory changes.

The Compliance Crew Training Ground:
- A captain ensures the crew is trained for efficient operations. Leaders establish the "Compliance Crew Training Ground," providing comprehensive training programs to equip employees with the knowledge and skills needed to navigate within legal boundaries.
- Develop training initiatives that cover all aspects of compliance relevant to different job roles. The Compliance Crew Training Ground ensures that every team member is well-versed in compliance requirements. Much like a captain ensuring the crew is trained, your leadership educates the team for effective compliance.

Harboring in the Port of Audits and Assessments:
- A captain harbors in a safe port for thorough inspection. Leaders anchor in the "Port of Audits and Assessments," conducting regular evaluations to ensure that the organization's compliance strategies are effective and up-to-date.
- Establish a robust auditing process to assess compliance levels. Harboring in the Port of Audits and Assessments ensures that the organization is continually refining and improving its compliance strategies. Like a captain inspecting a safe port, your leadership conducts thorough assessments of compliance effectiveness.

The Beacon of Internal Controls:
- A captain relies on beacons for navigation in the dark. Leaders establish the "Beacon of Internal Controls," implementing internal mechanisms and controls that guide the organization through the complexities of compliance.
- Develop and implement internal controls to ensure adherence to compliance strategies. The Beacon of Internal Controls illuminates the path, minimizing the risk of deviation from established compliance practices.

The role of management in compliance culture.

Comparable to a captain controlling a transport through misleading waters, this analogical direct investigates how adeptly grasping the part of administration in compliance culture contributes to smooth cruising, making positive waves inside the organizational scene.

The Helm of Ethical Direction:
- A captain uses the helm to steer the ship in the right direction. Leaders take on the "Helm of Ethical Direction," guiding the organization with a strong commitment to ethical practices and compliance.
- Set a clear ethical direction for the organization, emphasizing the importance of compliance in every decision and action. The Helm of Ethical Direction ensures that the organization sails towards a destination of integrity.

Charting the Course of Compliance Values:
- A captain charts the course on a map. Leaders chart the "Course of Compliance Values," outlining the core values and principles that define the organization's commitment to compliance.
- Clearly communicate and embed compliance values into the organizational culture. Charting the Course of Compliance Values ensures that every decision aligns with the principles of compliance. Similar to a captain charting a course, your leadership defines the path with compliance values.

Setting Sails of Accountability:
- A captain ensures every crew member is accountable for their duties. Leaders set sails of "Accountability," establishing a culture where every individual is responsible for upholding compliance standards.
- Implement accountability mechanisms and ensure consequences for non-compliance are clear. Setting Sails of Accountability ensures that everyone in the organization plays a role in maintaining compliance. Much like a captain ensuring crew accountability, your leadership fosters responsibility for compliance.

The Navigation Instruments of Training and Communication:
- A captain uses navigation instruments for accurate course plotting. Leaders utilize the "Navigation Instruments of Training and Communication," ensuring that the entire crew is well-trained and informed about compliance requirements.
- Develop comprehensive training programs and maintain open communication channels. The Navigation Instruments of Training and Communication ensure that everyone in the organization is aware of and understands compliance standards. Like a captain using navigation instruments, your leadership provides the tools for understanding and adhering to compliance.

Harboring in the Port of Transparent Leadership:
- A captain harbors in a safe port for transparency. Leaders anchor in the "Port of Transparent Leadership," fostering a culture where transparency about compliance efforts is paramount.
- Communicate openly about compliance initiatives and progress. Harboring in the Port of Transparent Leadership ensures that the organization builds trust with stakeholders through clear communication about compliance practices. Similar to a captain anchoring in a safe port, your leadership promotes transparency in compliance.

Chapter **20**

The Pillars of Trust
Building and maintaining trust.

Leaders with the Captain Mariner Mindset understand that building and maintaining trust is the anchor that stabilizes the ship and ensures smooth sailing. Similar to a captain earning the trust of the crew, this analogical guide explores how adeptly embracing the role of building and maintaining trust contributes to positive waves within the organizational landscape.

The Captain's Promise:
- A captain's promise assures the crew of safety and sound navigation. Leaders embody "The Captain's Promise," making commitments that foster trust among the team members.
- Clearly articulate values, expectations, and commitments. The Captain's Promise ensures that the organization sails with a foundation of trust, built on the leader's unwavering commitment to integrity and accountability. Like a captain assuring the crew, your leadership builds trust through promises kept.

Navigating Storms with Open Communication:
- A captain communicates openly during storms for crew reassurance. Leaders navigate storms with "Open Communication," fostering an environment where honest and transparent dialogue is encouraged, especially during challenging times.
- Establish open communication channels and encourage feedback. Navigating Storms with Open Communication ensures that the organization weathers challenges with trust intact, as the crew remains informed and reassured. Similar to a captain communicating in storms, your leadership promotes open and honest dialogue.

Trust as the Compass of Decision-Making:
- A captain relies on a compass for decision-making. Leaders use "Trust as the Compass of Decision-Making," ensuring that every choice aligns with the principles of trustworthiness and ethical conduct.
- Evaluate decisions based on their impact on trust. Trust as the Compass of Decision-Making ensures that the organization navigates its course with integrity, reinforcing trust among stakeholders. Like a captain using a compass, your leadership guides decisions with trust as a primary consideration.

Crew Unity in Trustful Waters:
- A united crew thrives in trustful waters. Leaders foster "Crew Unity in Trustful Waters," promoting collaboration and camaraderie built on trust among team members.
- Encourage teamwork and create an environment where individuals trust one another. Crew Unity in Trustful Waters ensures that the organization sails with a united front, as trust among team members enhances productivity and morale. Much like a captain fostering crew unity, your leadership builds a trusting and collaborative team.

The Trust Lighthouse in the Port of Accountability:
- A captain harbors in a safe port marked by a lighthouse. Leaders anchor in the "Trust Lighthouse in the Port of Accountability," where accountability and responsibility are emphasized to strengthen trust.
- Establish clear expectations and hold individuals accountable. The Trust Lighthouse in the Port of Accountability ensures that the organization harbors in an environment where trust is built on the foundation of individual responsibility. Similar to a captain anchoring in a safe port, your leadership promotes accountability for trust.

Trust as the Wind in the Sails of Innovation:
- A captain uses wind to propel the ship forward. Leaders leverage "Trust as the Wind in the Sails of Innovation," recognizing that trust fuels a culture of creativity and forward-thinking.
- Encourage a culture where trust allows individuals to take calculated risks and innovate. Trust as the Wind in the Sails of Innovation ensures that the organization sails into uncharted territories with confidence and creativity. Like a captain using wind for propulsion, your leadership propels innovation through a foundation of trust.

The impact of trust on team performance.

Within the endless ocean of viable administration, pioneers with the Captain Sailor Attitude get it that believe acts as the motor impelling the sails of high-performance groups. Comparable to a captain depending on a well-functioning motor for smooth cruising, this analogical direct investigates how adeptly grasping the affect of believe on group execution contributes to positive waves inside the organizational scene.

The Engine Room of Trust:
- A ship's engine powers its movement. Leaders become the stewards of "The Engine Room of Trust," recognizing that trust is the driving force behind team performance.
- Cultivate an environment where trust is prioritized. The Engine Room of Trust ensures that the team's performance is propelled by a robust foundation of mutual trust among its members. Like a captain maintaining a well-functioning engine, your leadership fosters trust as the powerhouse of team performance.

Fueling Collaboration and Coordination:
- A ship's engine ensures synchronized movement. Leaders understand that trust is the fuel that enables "Collaboration and Coordination." Just as a well-tuned engine ensures harmonious movements, trust fosters seamless collaboration and coordination within the team.
- Foster an atmosphere of trust where team members feel confident in each other's abilities. Fueling Collaboration and Coordination with trust ensures that the team moves forward cohesively, achieving goals with synchronized effort. Similar to a captain relying on a smoothly running engine, your leadership powers teamwork through trust.

Navigating Storms with Trust at the Helm:
- A reliable engine aids navigation through storms. Leaders guide the team through challenges with "Trust at the Helm," recognizing that during turbulent times, trust is the reliable force that helps navigate stormy waters.
- Reinforce trust during challenging periods, ensuring that the team navigates through uncertainties with confidence.
  Trust at the Helm ensures that even in difficult situations, the team maintains its course with resilience. Like a captain steering through storms, your leadership relies on trust to guide the team through challenges.

Efficient Resource Utilization Powered by Trust:
- An optimized engine ensures efficient use of resources. Leaders channel "Efficient Resource Utilization Powered by Trust," recognizing that trust minimizes friction and maximizes the efficient utilization of team resources.
- Foster a culture where trust allows for streamlined processes and effective resource allocation. Efficient Resource Utilization Powered by Trust ensures that the team operates at its peak, making the most of available resources. Much like a captain optimizing engine performance, your leadership maximizes team efficiency through trust.

Rebuilding trust after it's broken.

Within the tremendous ocean of compelling administration, pioneers with the Captain Sailor Mentality get it that believe, once broken, requires a fastidious approach to rebuilding. Comparative to a captain exploring through challenging waters, this analogical direct explores how adeptly grasping the method of revamping believe after it's broken contributes to positive waves inside the organizational scene.

The Salvage Operation:
- When a ship faces damage, a salvage operation is initiated. Leaders become the captains of "The Salvage Operation," recognizing that rebuilding trust requires a strategic and concerted effort.
- Assess the extent of the trust breach, identify key areas for improvement, and initiate a comprehensive plan for rebuilding trust. The Salvage Operation ensures that trust is meticulously restored, much like a captain navigating through the aftermath of a storm.

Mending the Sails of Communication:
- Damaged sails impede a ship's progress.
  Leaders focus on "Mending the Sails of Communication," recognizing that open and honest dialogue is essential in the trust restoration process.
- Establish transparent communication channels to address concerns, apologize for any wrongdoing, and articulate a clear path forward. Mending the Sails of Communication ensures that the organization sails forward with repaired sails, strengthened by improved communication. Like a captain repairing sails, your leadership restores trust through transparent and effective communication.

The Lighthouse of Accountability:
- A lighthouse guides a ship to safety. Leaders become the beacons in "The Lighthouse of Accountability," ensuring that accountability is a guiding light throughout the trust restoration journey.
- Set clear expectations, hold individuals accountable for their actions, and implement measures to prevent future trust breaches. The Lighthouse of Accountability ensures that the organization navigates toward trust with a steadfast commitment to responsibility. Much like a captain relying on a lighthouse for safe navigation, your leadership guides trust restoration through a commitment to accountability.

Charting a New Course of Consistency:
- A captain charts a new course after overcoming challenges. Leaders focus on "Charting a New Course of Consistency," recognizing that rebuilding trust requires a commitment to consistent and reliable behavior.
- Demonstrate consistency in actions, decisions, and communication. Charting a New Course of Consistency ensures that the organization sails toward renewed trust on a stable and predictable course. Similar to a captain navigating a new course, your leadership guides the team with unwavering consistency.

Navigating the Depths of Empathy:
- In challenging waters, empathy becomes the compass. Leaders navigate the depths of "Empathy," understanding that acknowledging and understanding the feelings of those affected by the trust breach is crucial.
- Demonstrate sincere empathy, actively listen to concerns, and take steps to address the emotional impact of the breach. Navigating the Depths of Empathy ensures that the organization sails toward trust renewal with a deep understanding of the emotional aspects involved.

Chapter **21**

Sailing in the Digital Age
Embracing digital transformation.

In the tremendous ocean of viable administration, pioneers with the Captain Sailor Mentality recognize the transformative control of innovation. Comparable to a captain exploring through strange waters, this analogical direct investigates how adeptly grasping advanced change contributes to positive waves inside the organizational scene.

The Technological Compass:
- A ship relies on a compass for navigation. Leaders become the stewards of "The Technological Compass," acknowledging that digital transformation serves as the guiding force for organizational direction.
- Understand the digital landscape, identify technological trends, and chart a course that aligns with the organization's goals. The Technological Compass ensures that the organization navigates into the future with a clear understanding of technological advancements. Like a captain relying on a compass, your leadership guides the team through the digital landscape.

Sailing the Cloud Seas:
- Cloud technology enables seamless navigation. Leaders focus on "Sailing the Cloud Seas," recognizing that cloud solutions provide a flexible and scalable infrastructure for organizational operations.
- Embrace cloud-based technologies to enhance collaboration, data storage, and accessibility. Sailing the Cloud Seas ensures that the organization sails with agility, leveraging the benefits of cloud technology. Similar to a captain utilizing favorable winds, your leadership harnesses the power of the cloud for organizational efficiency.

Navigating the Data Waves:
- A captain analyzes ocean currents for efficient navigation. Leaders become proficient at "Navigating the Data Waves," understanding the significance of data in making informed decisions.
- Implement data-driven strategies, gather actionable insights, and ensure data security. Navigating the Data Waves ensures that the organization steers with precision, leveraging data for strategic decision-making. Like a captain analyzing currents, your leadership navigates through the sea of information to guide the team effectively.

Digital Crew Empowerment:
- A well-trained crew enhances the ship's capabilities. Leaders prioritize "Digital Crew Empowerment," recognizing that a skilled workforce is essential for successful digital transformation.
- Invest in digital literacy training, encourage continuous learning, and foster a culture that embraces technological advancements. Digital Crew Empowerment ensures that the organization's workforce is equipped to navigate the digital landscape. Similar to a captain ensuring a skilled crew, your leadership empowers the team with digital skills.

The Cybersecurity Fortress:
- A fortress protects the ship from external threats. Leaders establish "The Cybersecurity Fortress," understanding the importance of safeguarding digital assets from cyber threats.
- Implement robust cybersecurity measures, educate the team on security best practices, and regularly update defenses. The Cybersecurity Fortress ensures that the organization sails securely through the digital realm. Like a captain fortifying against external threats, your leadership safeguards the digital integrity of the organization.

Digital Innovation as the Wind in the Sails:
- Just as wind propels sails, digital innovation drives organizational progress. Leaders leverage "Digital Innovation as the Wind in the Sails," recognizing that innovative technologies propel the organization forward.
- Encourage a culture of innovation, invest in emerging technologies, and explore digital solutions for business challenges. Digital Innovation as the Wind in the Sails ensures that the organization sails into the future with a pioneering spirit. Similar to a captain harnessing wind for propulsion, your leadership propels the team through the waters of digital innovation.

The role of technology in modern management.

In the endless ocean of viable administration, pioneers with the Captain Sailor Attitude get it the significant part of innovation in directing the transport of advanced administration. Comparative to a captain adeptly utilizing navigational apparatuses, this analogical direct investigates how innovation gets to be the compass for making positive waves inside the organizational scene.

The Digital Sextant:
- A sextant guides navigation by celestial bodies. Leaders become the navigators with "The Digital Sextant," recognizing that technology acts as a precision tool for plotting the course of modern management.
- Embrace digital tools for analytics, data interpretation, and decision-making. The Digital Sextant ensures that leaders navigate the complexities of modern management with precision, just as a captain relies on a sextant for accurate navigation.

Steering with Artificial Intelligence Winds:
- Winds propel a ship, and AI propels efficiency.
Leaders focus on "Steering with Artificial Intelligence Winds," acknowledging that AI enhances decision-making, automation, and operational efficiency.
- Integrate AI solutions for data analysis, process automation, and predictive insights. Steering with Artificial Intelligence Winds ensures that the organization sails efficiently through the modern management landscape. Similar to a captain adjusting sails to the wind, your leadership harnesses the power of AI for enhanced efficiency.

Sailing the Data Seas:
- Data is the sea of information that surrounds the organization. Leaders become adept sailors on "The Data Seas," recognizing the importance of collecting, analyzing, and leveraging data for informed decision-making.
- Implement robust data management strategies, utilize analytics tools, and ensure data-driven decision-making. Sailing the Data Seas ensures that the organization navigates with a clear understanding of the information landscape. Like a captain charting a course through the seas, your leadership steers through the vast ocean of organizational data.

The Connectivity Compass:
- Connectivity is the compass that guides communication. Leaders focus on "The Connectivity Compass," understanding that modern management thrives on seamless communication and collaboration.
- Utilize collaborative platforms, communication tools, and ensure a connected digital ecosystem. The Connectivity Compass ensures that the organization maintains effective communication channels. Similar to a captain relying on a compass for direction, your leadership ensures connectivity for smooth communication.

Automation as the Engine Room:
- The engine room powers the ship; automation powers efficiency. Leaders prioritize "Automation as the Engine Room," recognizing that automated processes enhance productivity and reduce manual workload.

- Implement workflow automation, utilize robotic process automation (RPA), and streamline repetitive tasks. Automation as the Engine Room ensures that the organization sails with increased efficiency. Like a captain optimizing the engine for peak performance, your leadership leverages automation for organizational efficiency.

Balancing human and digital resources.

In the endless ocean of compelling administration, pioneers with the Captain Sailor Mentality recognize the sensitive move between human and computerized assets. Comparable to a captain exploring differing group flow, this analogical direct investigates how adeptly adjusting human and advanced assets makes positive waves inside the organizational scene.

The Crew Ensemble:
- A ship's crew is a diverse ensemble. Leaders become conductors orchestrating "The Crew Ensemble," acknowledging the importance of harmonizing both human and digital resources.
- Understand the unique strengths of human and digital resources, fostering a collaborative environment where both elements complement each other. The Crew Ensemble ensures that the organization sails with a synchronized balance. Similar to a captain orchestrating a diverse crew, your leadership harmonizes human and digital resources.

Digital Deckhands and Human Helmsmen:
- Deckhands perform routine tasks, while helmsmen steer the ship. Leaders focus on "Digital Deckhands and Human Helmsmen," recognizing the distinct roles that automated processes (digital deckhands) and human decision-makers (human helmsmen) play in steering the organization.
- Delegate routine tasks to automated processes, allowing human resources to focus on strategic decision-making. Digital Deckhands and Human Helmsmen ensure that the organization navigates efficiently with a balanced delegation of tasks. Like a captain delegating responsibilities, your leadership optimizes efficiency with a balanced approach.

Navigating Emotional Currents:
- Emotional currents impact the crew's morale. Leaders navigate through "Emotional Currents," understanding the human aspect of the workforce and how emotions influence productivity.
- Implement digital tools that enhance emotional intelligence, prioritize employee well-being, and foster a positive work culture.
  Navigating Emotional Currents ensures that the organization sails with a crew in high spirits. Similar to a captain understanding the crew's emotions, your leadership navigates through the emotional landscape of the workforce.

The Digital Compass and Human Intuition:
- A compass provides direction, and human intuition guides decision-making. Leaders prioritize "The Digital Compass and Human Intuition," understanding that while digital tools provide data-driven insights, human intuition is crucial for strategic decision-making.
- Utilize digital analytics tools for data-driven insights, while relying on human intuition for complex decision-making. The Digital Compass and Human Intuition ensure that the organization navigates with a well-balanced blend of data and intuition. Like a captain combining technology with instinct, your leadership leverages both digital and human capabilities.

Chapter **22**

Wellness on Waves
Workplace wellness initiatives.

Pioneers with the Captain Sailor Attitude get it the significance of a solid and persuaded group. Comparative to a captain guaranteeing the well-being of the ship's team, this analogical direct investigates how working environment wellness activities make positive waves inside the organizational scene.

The Wellness Wind in the Sails:
- A ship propelled by a favorable wind. Leaders become the wind in "The Wellness Wind in the Sails," acknowledging that wellness initiatives provide the energy needed for the organization to sail smoothly.
- Implement holistic wellness programs, focusing on physical health, mental well-being, and work-life balance. The Wellness Wind in the Sails ensures that the organization sails with the energy and vigor derived from a healthy workforce. Like a captain harnessing favorable winds, your leadership propels the team through the waters of well-being.

Navigating Mental Health Tides:
- Mental health as the ebb and flow of tides. Leaders navigate "Mental Health Tides," recognizing the impact of mental well-being on the overall health of the crew.
- Establish mental health support programs, encourage open conversations, and create a stigma-free environment. Navigating Mental Health Tides ensures that the organization sails with a mentally resilient crew. Similar to a captain navigating through changing tides, your leadership steers the team through the waters of mental well-being.

Crew Nutrition and Nourishment:
- A well-fed crew is a strong crew. Leaders focus on "Crew Nutrition and Nourishment," understanding that proper nourishment is vital for sustained energy and performance.
- Provide healthy food options, promote nutritional awareness, and encourage mindful eating habits. Crew Nutrition and Nourishment ensure that the organization sails with a crew fueled for optimal performance. Like a captain ensuring the crew is well-fed, your leadership provides the nourishment needed for success.

Physical Fitness as the Ship's Engine:
- The ship's engine powers its movement. Leaders prioritize "Physical Fitness as the Ship's Engine," recognizing that a physically fit workforce is the engine driving organizational productivity.
- Establish fitness programs, encourage regular exercise, and create a culture that values physical well-being. Physical Fitness as the Ship's Engine ensures that the organization sails with a workforce that is physically resilient and ready for the challenges ahead. Similar to a captain maintaining the ship's engine, your leadership keeps the workforce physically fit for peak performance.

Sailing the Waters of Work-Life Balance:
- Work-life balance as the equilibrium of tides. Leaders focus on "Sailing the Waters of Work-Life Balance," understanding that a balanced approach enhances both individual well-being and organizational productivity.
- Promote flexible work arrangements, encourage time-off policies, and foster a culture that values the harmony between work and personal life.
  Sailing the Waters of Work-Life Balance ensures that the organization navigates with a crew that is not only productive but also fulfilled in their personal lives. Like a

captain steering through balanced waters, your leadership maintains the equilibrium of work and life.

Harvesting the Fruits of Employee Engagement:
- A bountiful harvest from well-cared-for plants. Leaders prioritize "Harvesting the Fruits of Employee Engagement," recognizing that engaged and motivated employees contribute to a flourishing and productive workplace.
- Implement engagement initiatives, recognize achievements, and create opportunities for employee growth and development. Harvesting the Fruits of Employee Engagement ensures that the organization sails with a crew that is invested in its success. Similar to a captain enjoying the fruits of a well-tended garden, your leadership reaps the benefits of an engaged and motivated workforce.

Work-life balance.

In the endless ocean of viable administration, pioneers with the Captain Sailor Mentality recognize the noteworthiness of work-life adjust as the compass directing the dispatch of organizational victory. Comparable to a captain guaranteeing a concordant travel, this analogical direct investigates how prioritizing work-life adjust makes positive waves inside the organizational scene.

Balancing the Crew Quarters:
- A well-organized and comfortable crew quarters. Leaders focus on "Balancing the Crew Quarters," understanding that a balanced workspace contributes to the overall well-being of the crew.
- Establish a conducive work environment, promote ergonomic practices, and encourage breaks for relaxation. Balancing the Crew Quarters ensures that the organization sails with a crew that is physically and mentally comfortable. Like a captain ensuring comfortable crew quarters, your leadership fosters an environment conducive to work-life harmony.

The Work-Life Navigation Chart:
- A navigation chart plotting the course through work and personal life. Leaders become the navigators with "The Work-Life Navigation Chart," recognizing the importance of clear guidelines for navigating the waters of professional and personal responsibilities.
- Establish clear expectations, promote flexible work arrangements, and encourage time management strategies. The Work-Life Navigation Chart ensures that the organization sails with a crew equipped with a clear route for balancing work and personal life. Similar to a captain relying on a navigation chart, your leadership provides a roadmap for work-life harmony.

Flexible Sails for Adaptable Winds:
- Sails that can adjust to changing winds. Leaders prioritize "Flexible Sails for Adaptable Winds," understanding that flexibility is crucial for accommodating the changing needs of the crew.
- Implement flexible work hours, remote work options, and adaptable project timelines. Flexible Sails for Adaptable Winds ensures that the organization sails with a crew that can navigate through the winds of personal and professional demands.
Like a captain adjusting sails to the wind, your leadership adapts to the evolving needs of the workforce.

Harmonizing the Crew's Rhythms:
- The synchronization of crew tasks and personal rhythms. Leaders focus on "Harmonizing the Crew's Rhythms," recognizing the importance of aligning work schedules with the natural rhythms of the crew.
- Implement staggered work hours, consider individual preferences, and promote a culture that respects personal time. Harmonizing the Crew's Rhythms ensures that the organization sails with a crew in sync with their natural energy and productivity peaks.

Similar to a captain harmonizing tasks with the crew's rhythms, your leadership aligns work schedules with individual preferences.

Dealing with burnout and stress.

Pioneers with the Captain Sailor Mentality get it the turbulent waters of burnout and push and the affect on the crew's well-being. Comparative to a captain directing the dispatch through storms, this analogical direct investigates how compelling pioneers can oversee burnout and push to form positive waves inside the organizational scene.

The Compassionate Harbor:

- A safe harbor for crew recovery. Leaders focus on "The Compassionate Harbor," recognizing the importance of providing a supportive and compassionate environment for the crew during times of burnout and stress.
- Establish open communication channels, encourage seeking support, and offer resources for mental well-being. The Compassionate Harbor ensures that the organization sails with a crew that feels supported and cared for. Like a captain providing a safe harbor during storms, your leadership offers a supportive space for team members facing burnout and stress.

Storm Preparedness Training:

- Equipping the crew to face storms. Leaders prioritize "Storm Preparedness Training," understanding that proactive measures can help the crew navigate through challenging times.
- Provide stress management workshops, encourage resilience-building activities, and foster a culture that values mental health. Storm Preparedness Training ensures that the organization sails with a crew equipped to face and manage stress effectively. Similar to a captain preparing the crew for storms, your leadership provides tools and resources for stress resilience.

Balancing Workload and Navigation:

- Distributing workload to navigate smoothly. Leaders focus on "Balancing Workload and Navigation," understanding that an imbalanced workload can lead to burnout.
- Regularly assess and adjust workloads, promote realistic expectations, and encourage open communication about workload concerns. Balancing Workload and Navigation ensures that the organization sails with a crew that manages responsibilities without succumbing to burnout.
  Like a captain adjusting the ship's load for smooth navigation, your leadership maintains a balanced workload for the team.

Restoring the Sails of Energy:

- Renewing the sails for continued journey. Leaders prioritize "Restoring the Sails of Energy," recognizing the need for periodic breaks and rejuvenation to prevent burnout.
- Encourage the use of vacation time, promote breaks during intense work periods, and discourage excessive overtime. Restoring the Sails of Energy ensures that the organization sails with a crew that is energized and ready for the journey ahead. Similar to a captain renewing sails for continued journey, your leadership values and encourages breaks for the team.

Chapter **23**

Financial Tides
Fiscal responsibility and budget management.

Comparable to a captain managing the ship's accounts, this analogical direct investigates how successful pioneers can hone financial duty and budget administration to form positive waves inside the organizational scene.

The Financial Navigation Chart:
- A navigation chart for financial waters. Leaders become navigators with "The Financial Navigation Chart," recognizing the importance of clear guidelines and strategic planning for navigating the complex financial currents.
- Establish a comprehensive budget, regularly assess financial goals, and implement strategic financial planning. The Financial Navigation Chart ensures that the organization sails with a clear financial roadmap. Like a captain relying on a navigation chart, your leadership provides a strategic plan for financial success.

Balancing the Budget Sails:
- Adjusting sails for balanced navigation. Leaders focus on "Balancing the Budget Sails," understanding that a well-allocated budget is crucial for navigating financial challenges.
- Monitor and adjust budget allocations, prioritize essential expenditures, and promote a culture of cost-consciousness. Balancing the Budget Sails ensures that the organization sails with a well-managed budget, minimizing financial risks. Similar to a captain adjusting sails for balanced navigation, your leadership allocates resources strategically for financial stability.

Financial Storm Preparedness:
- Equipping the ship for financial storms. Leaders prioritize "Financial Storm Preparedness," understanding that proactive financial measures can help the organization weather economic challenges.
- Establish contingency funds, conduct regular financial risk assessments, and implement strategies for financial resilience. Financial Storm Preparedness ensures that the organization sails with a financial plan prepared to weather unforeseen challenges. Like a captain preparing the ship for storms, your leadership equips the organization for financial resilience.

Navigating the Tides of Cost-Efficiency:
- Efficiently navigating through cost currents. Leaders focus on "Navigating the Tides of Cost-Efficiency," recognizing that optimizing costs is essential for financial sustainability.
- Implement cost-cutting measures, assess the return on investment for projects, and promote efficiency in resource utilization. Navigating the Tides of Cost-Efficiency ensures that the organization sails with a crew mindful of financial implications. Similar to a captain navigating through cost currents, your leadership optimizes expenses for fiscal responsibility.

Harvesting Financial Growth:
- Cultivating a bountiful financial harvest. Leaders prioritize "Harvesting Financial Growth," understanding that strategic investments can contribute to the organization's financial prosperity.
- Identify opportunities for financial growth, assess investment options, and cultivate a culture that values long-term financial sustainability. Harvesting Financial Growth ensures that the organization sails with a crew focused on cultivating financial success.

Like a captain cultivating a bountiful harvest, your leadership strategically invests for financial growth.

Financial Auditing for Smooth Sailing:
- Regularly auditing the ship's financial health. Leaders prioritize "Financial Auditing for Smooth Sailing," recognizing the importance of regular financial assessments for maintaining financial integrity.
- Conduct regular financial audits, address discrepancies promptly, and ensure compliance with financial regulations. Financial Auditing for Smooth Sailing ensures that the organization sails with a financially sound foundation. Similar to a captain regularly auditing the ship's health, your leadership assesses the organization's financial well-being.

Financial planning and analysis.

Comparative to a captain charting a course through eccentric oceans, this analogical direct investigates how viable budgetary arranging and investigation make positive waves inside the organizational scene.

The Financial Navigation Chart:
- A detailed navigation chart for financial waters. Leaders focus on "The Financial Navigation Chart," recognizing the need for a comprehensive plan to navigate the complexities of financial management.
- Develop a strategic financial plan, incorporating budgeting, forecasting, and risk analysis. The Financial Navigation Chart ensures that the organization sails with a clear direction and understanding of its financial landscape. Like a captain relying on a navigation chart, your leadership provides a roadmap for financial success.

Setting Sail with Budgetary Discipline:
- Budgeting as the disciplined setting of sails. Leaders prioritize "Setting Sail with Budgetary Discipline," understanding that disciplined budgeting is the key to effective financial management.
- Establish a transparent budgeting process, track expenses rigorously, and make informed decisions based on budgetary constraints. Setting Sail with Budgetary Discipline ensures that the organization sails with financial sails set in a disciplined manner. Similar to a captain setting sails with discipline, your leadership steers the organization with financial rigor.

Navigating Economic Currents:
- Economic currents impacting the ship's trajectory. Leaders focus on "Navigating Economic Currents," recognizing the need to stay informed and adapt financial strategies to changing economic conditions.
- Regularly assess market trends, adjust financial plans based on economic forecasts, and implement contingency measures. Navigating Economic Currents ensures that the organization sails with financial strategies aligned with prevailing economic conditions. Like a captain adjusting course to navigate currents, your leadership adapts financial strategies to economic changes.

Riding the Waves of Profitability:
- Profits as the waves propelling the ship forward.
  Leaders prioritize "Riding the Waves of Profitability," understanding that sustained profits are essential for organizational growth.
- Implement strategies to enhance revenue streams, control costs, and maximize profitability. Riding the Waves of Profitability ensures that the organization sails with a financial momentum driving its success. Similar to a captain riding waves for propulsion, your leadership leverages profits for organizational advancement.

Risk Management: Weathering Financial Storms:
- Financial risks as unpredictable storms. Leaders focus on "Risk Management: Weathering Financial Storms," recognizing the need to identify, assess, and mitigate financial risks proactively.
- Conduct regular risk assessments, implement risk mitigation strategies, and maintain a contingency fund. Risk Management: Weathering Financial Storms ensures that the organization sails with resilience against potential financial adversities. Like a captain navigating through storms, your leadership steers through financial risks with foresight.

Cost-cutting without compromising quality.

In the tremendous ocean of compelling administration, pioneers with the Captain Sailor Attitude get it the fragile adjust of trimming costs without compromising the quality of the voyage. Comparative to a captain optimizing assets for effective cruising, this analogical direct investigates how compelling cost-cutting hones make positive waves inside the organizational scene.

The Frugal Navigation Chart:
- A strategic navigation chart for cost-efficient sailing. Leaders focus on "The Frugal Navigation Chart," recognizing the need for a meticulous plan to navigate the waters of cost-cutting without sacrificing quality.
- Conduct a thorough cost analysis, identify non-essential expenses, and develop a strategic cost-cutting plan. The Frugal Navigation Chart ensures that the organization sails with a lean budget while maintaining quality standards. Like a captain navigating with a frugal chart, your leadership guides the organization through efficient cost-cutting.

Trimming Excess Cargo:
- Unloading unnecessary cargo for streamlined sailing. Leaders prioritize "Trimming Excess Cargo," understanding that eliminating non-essential expenditures contributes to cost efficiency.
- Evaluate all expenses, identify redundant processes, and cut unnecessary costs without compromising core functions. Trimming Excess Cargo ensures that the organization sails with a lighter load, promoting efficiency without sacrificing quality. Similar to a captain removing excess cargo for streamlined sailing, your leadership eliminates unnecessary expenses for organizational efficiency.

Navigating the Seas of Operational Efficiency:
- Operational efficiency as favorable winds for cost-effectiveness. Leaders focus on "Navigating the Seas of Operational Efficiency," recognizing that streamlined processes lead to cost savings without compromising quality.
- Implement lean methodologies, automate repetitive tasks, and optimize workflows to enhance operational efficiency. Navigating the Seas of Operational Efficiency ensures that the organization sails with cost-effective operations while maintaining quality standards.
  Like a captain navigating with favorable winds, your leadership leverages operational efficiency for cost savings.

Investing in Sustainable Fuel:
- Sustainable fuel for enduring cost-effectiveness. Leaders prioritize "Investing in Sustainable Fuel," understanding that long-term cost savings come from investing in sustainable and efficient solutions.
- Identify eco-friendly and cost-effective technologies, implement energy-efficient practices, and invest in sustainable solutions for long-term savings. Investing in Sustainable Fuel ensures that the organization sails with enduring cost-effectiveness without compromising quality. Similar to a captain investing in sustainable fuel for

enduring journeys, your leadership chooses cost-effective solutions with long-term benefits.

Green Sailing: Environmental Responsibility Implementing sustainable practices.

In the tremendous ocean of successful administration, pioneers with the Captain Sailor Mentality get it the significance of controlling their organizations towards maintainability, much like a captain ensuring the ship's travel incorporates a positive affect on the environment. This analogical direct investigates how actualizing feasible hones makes positive waves inside the organizational scene.

The Eco-Friendly Navigation Chart:

- A sustainable navigation chart for responsible sailing. Leaders focus on "The Eco-Friendly Navigation Chart," recognizing the need for a comprehensive plan to navigate the corporate waters while minimizing environmental impact.
- Develop and implement sustainability policies, set environmental goals, and integrate eco-friendly practices into daily operations. The Eco-Friendly Navigation Chart ensures that the organization sails with a clear commitment to sustainability.
  Like a captain navigating with an eco-friendly chart, your leadership guides the organization towards responsible practices.

Reducing Carbon Emissions: Sailing with a Lighter Environmental Footprint:

- Reducing carbon emissions for an environmentally lighter voyage. Leaders prioritize "Reducing Carbon Emissions," understanding the significant impact of carbon neutrality on environmental sustainability.
- Implement energy-efficient technologies, reduce unnecessary travel, and invest in renewable energy sources. Reducing Carbon Emissions ensures that the organization sails with a lighter environmental footprint, contributing to a sustainable future. Similar to a captain adopting measures for carbon neutrality, your leadership steers the organization towards reducing its environmental impact.

Recycling as the Wind in the Corporate Sails:

- Recycling as a source of renewable energy for organizational growth. Leaders focus on "Recycling as the Wind in the Corporate Sails," recognizing the value of repurposing resources for sustained corporate vitality.
- Establish recycling programs, encourage the use of recycled materials, and minimize waste generation. Recycling as the Wind in the Corporate Sails ensures that the organization sails with a commitment to resource efficiency and environmental stewardship. Like a captain harnessing wind for sail propulsion, your leadership utilizes recycled resources for sustained corporate growth.

Green Procurement: Harvesting Sustainable Resources:

- Green procurement as harvesting sustainable resources for the ship's journey. Leaders prioritize "Green Procurement: Harvesting Sustainable Resources," understanding the impact of responsible sourcing on overall sustainability.
- Source products and materials from environmentally responsible suppliers, prioritize eco-friendly certifications, and support sustainable production practices. Green Procurement ensures that the organization sails with resources harvested responsibly. Similar to a captain procuring sustainable resources for the ship, your leadership makes responsible choices in sourcing.

Ocean Advocacy: Protecting the Corporate Seas:

- Ocean advocacy as protecting the corporate seas. Leaders focus on "Ocean Advocacy: Protecting the Corporate Seas," understanding the importance of supporting environmental causes and initiatives.
- Engage in environmental conservation projects, support marine protection efforts, and contribute to sustainability-focused organizations. Ocean Advocacy ensures that the organization sails with a commitment to protecting the environment. Like a captain

advocating for the seas, your leadership supports initiatives that protect the corporate environment.

The role of management in corporate social responsibility.
Within the tremendous ocean of viable administration, pioneers with the Captain Sailor Attitude get it the pivotal part of directing their organizations towards Corporate Social Obligation (CSR), much like a captain guaranteeing the ship's travel emphatically impacts society. This analogical direct investigates how the part of administration in CSR makes positive waves inside the organizational and societal scene.

The Ethical Navigation Chart:
- An ethical navigation chart for socially responsible sailing. Leaders focus on "The Ethical Navigation Chart," recognizing the need for a comprehensive plan to navigate corporate waters while upholding ethical and socially responsible practices.
- Develop and implement CSR policies, align business strategies with social responsibility, and foster a culture that prioritizes ethical conduct. The Ethical Navigation Chart ensures that the organization sails with a clear commitment to CSR. Like a captain navigating with an ethical chart, your leadership guides the organization towards responsible and socially conscious practices.

Community Engagement: Anchoring in Social Contribution:
- Community engagement as anchoring in social contribution. Leaders prioritize "Community Engagement," understanding the importance of actively contributing to the communities in which the organization operates.
- Initiate community outreach programs, support local causes, and encourage employee volunteerism. Community Engagement ensures that the organization anchors in social contribution, positively impacting local communities. Similar to a captain anchoring in a harbor for community interaction, your leadership actively contributes to societal well-being.

Sustainable Partnerships: Navigating Collaborative Seas:
- Sustainable partnerships as navigating collaborative seas for societal benefit. Leaders focus on "Sustainable Partnerships," recognizing the power of collaboration with stakeholders to create positive societal impacts.
- Form partnerships with NGOs, governmental agencies, and other businesses to address societal challenges collaboratively. Sustainable Partnerships ensure that the organization sails with a commitment to collaborative initiatives.
  Like a captain navigating with partners for a joint voyage, your leadership collaborates for societal benefit.

Transparent Reporting: Clear Skies for Ethical Visibility:
- Transparent reporting as clear skies for ethical visibility. Leaders prioritize "Transparent Reporting," understanding the importance of openly communicating CSR efforts to stakeholders.
- Implement robust reporting mechanisms, share CSR initiatives transparently, and seek feedback from stakeholders. Transparent Reporting ensures that the organization sails with clear skies of ethical visibility, building trust with stakeholders. Similar to a captain navigating in clear skies, your leadership communicates CSR efforts openly for ethical visibility.

Measuring environmental impact.
In the vast sea of effective management, leaders with the Captain Mariner Mindset understand the importance of navigating the environmental impact of their organizations, much like a captain ensuring their ship's journey leaves positive waves on the environment. This analogical guide explores how measuring environmental impact creates positive waves within the organizational landscape.

The Sustainability Sextant: Navigating with Precision:
- A sustainability sextant for precise navigation. Leaders focus on "The Sustainability Sextant," recognizing the need for accurate tools to measure and navigate the environmental impact of the organization.
- Implement environmental impact assessment tools, conduct life cycle analyses, and set key performance indicators (KPIs) for sustainability. The Sustainability Sextant ensures that the organization sails with a clear understanding of its environmental impact. Like a captain navigating with a sextant, your leadership guides the organization with precision through environmental assessments.

Carbon Footprint as the Compass for Emission Reduction:
- Carbon footprint as the guiding compass for emission reduction. Leaders prioritize "Carbon Footprint as the Compass for Emission Reduction," understanding the significance of tracking and minimizing greenhouse gas emissions.
- Conduct a thorough carbon footprint assessment, set emission reduction targets, and implement strategies to minimize carbon emissions. Carbon Footprint as the Compass for Emission Reduction ensures that the organization sails with a commitment to reducing its environmental footprint. Similar to a captain steering by a compass, your leadership guides the organization towards emission reduction goals.

Oceanic Monitoring: Tracking Resource Usage:
- Oceanic monitoring as tracking resource usage for sustainable practices. Leaders focus on "Oceanic Monitoring: Tracking Resource Usage," recognizing the importance of monitoring resource consumption for sustainability.
- Track resource usage, including energy, water, and raw materials, implement resource-efficient technologies, and establish resource conservation initiatives. Oceanic Monitoring ensures that the organization sails with a mindful approach to resource usage. Like a captain monitoring the ocean for sustainable practices, your leadership tracks and optimizes resource consumption.

Eco-Performance Indicators: The North Star of Sustainability:
- Eco-performance indicators as the North Star guiding sustainability efforts. Leaders prioritize "Eco-Performance Indicators: The North Star of Sustainability," recognizing the need for clear metrics to guide environmental initiatives.
- Establish eco-performance indicators aligned with sustainability goals, regularly assess performance against these indicators, and adjust strategies accordingly. Eco-Performance Indicators ensure that the organization sails with a focus on continuous improvement in environmental performance. Similar to a captain navigating by the North Star, your leadership steers environmental efforts with clear indicators.

Chapter **24**

Customer Compass
Customer-centric management.

Within the tremendous ocean of viable administration, pioneers with the Captain Sailor Mentality get it the significance of controlling their organizations towards customer-centricity, much like a captain guaranteeing the travelers have a paramount and fulfilling voyage. This analogical direct investigates how grasping customer-centric administration makes positive waves inside the organizational scene.

The Compass of Customer-Centricity:
- A customer-centric compass for navigating organizational waters. Leaders focus on "The Compass of Customer-Centricity," recognizing that customer satisfaction guides the course of the entire organization.
- Instill a customer-centric culture, prioritize customer needs in decision-making, and integrate customer feedback into organizational strategies. The Compass of Customer-Centricity ensures that the organization sails with a clear focus on customer satisfaction.

  Like a captain relying on a compass for direction, your leadership navigates the organization with a customer-centric mindset.

Setting Sail with Customer Feedback:
- Customer feedback as the wind in the organizational sails. Leaders prioritize "Setting Sail with Customer Feedback," understanding that customer insights drive continuous improvement.
- Establish robust feedback mechanisms, actively listen to customer opinions, and use feedback to refine products, services, and processes. Setting Sail with Customer Feedback ensures that the organization sails with a constant breeze of customer-driven improvements. Similar to a captain adjusting sails based on the wind, your leadership adapts strategies based on customer feedback.

Smooth Seas: Seamless Customer Experiences:
- Seamless customer experiences for smooth sailing. Leaders focus on "Smooth Seas: Seamless Customer Experiences," understanding the importance of providing consistent and enjoyable interactions.
- Streamline customer touchpoints, ensure consistency across channels, and prioritize user-friendly interfaces.

  Smooth Seas ensures that the organization sails with a commitment to providing seamless and enjoyable experiences. Like a captain ensuring smooth seas for passengers, your leadership creates a journey marked by effortless customer interactions.

Customizing the Voyage: Personalization in Customer Service:
- Personalization as customizing the voyage for each passenger. Leaders prioritize "Customizing the Voyage: Personalization in Customer Service," recognizing the value of tailored experiences.
- Utilize data for personalized communication, offer customized solutions, and understand individual customer preferences. Customizing the Voyage ensures that the organization sails with a commitment to delivering personalized and attentive customer service. Similar to a captain customizing the voyage for passengers, your leadership tailors experiences to individual customer needs.

Anticipating Storms: Proactive Customer Service:
- Proactive customer service as anticipating storms before they arrive. Leaders focus on "Anticipating Storms: Proactive Customer Service," understanding the importance of identifying and addressing potential issues before they escalate.

- Implement predictive analytics, monitor customer behavior, and proactively address concerns. Anticipating Storms ensures that the organization sails with a commitment to preventing and mitigating potential customer challenges. Like a captain anticipating storms for passenger safety, your leadership addresses issues before they become significant challenges.

Crew Training: Empowering Frontline Teams for Customer Satisfaction:
- Crew training as empowering frontline teams for passenger satisfaction. Leaders prioritize "Crew Training: Empowering Frontline Teams for Customer Satisfaction," recognizing that empowered employees contribute to positive customer experiences.
- Invest in employee training, empower frontline teams to make customer-centric decisions, and foster a culture of service excellence. Crew Training ensures that the organization sails with a crew well-equipped to deliver exceptional customer service. Similar to a captain training the crew for passenger satisfaction, your leadership empowers employees to enhance customer experiences.

Building relationships with clients.

In the tremendous ocean of viable administration, pioneers with the Captain Sailor Mentality get it the significance of building solid connections with clients, much like a captain cultivating associations with travelers for a paramount travel. This analogical direct investigates how developing client connections makes positive waves inside the organizational scene.

The Nautical Handshake:
- The nautical handshake as the foundation of client relationships. Leaders focus on "The Nautical Handshake," recognizing that the initial greeting sets the tone for a successful journey.
- Prioritize a warm and personalized onboarding process, establish clear communication channels, and ensure clients feel welcomed from the outset. The Nautical Handshake ensures that the organization sails with a commitment to building strong and positive client connections. Like a captain's handshake conveying trust, your leadership sets the foundation for successful partnerships.

Charting the Course Together: Collaborative Goal-Setting:
- Collaborative goal-setting as charting the course together with clients. Leaders prioritize "Charting the Course Together: Collaborative Goal-Setting," recognizing the importance of aligning organizational objectives with client expectations.
- Engage clients in goal-setting discussions, understand their aspirations, and collaborate on strategies for mutual success. Charting the Course Together ensures that the organization sails with a shared vision, fostering strong and collaborative client relationships. Similar to a captain collaborating with passengers on the journey's course, your leadership aligns organizational goals with client expectations.

Smooth Sailing Through Communication Channels:
- Smooth sailing through communication channels for seamless interactions. Leaders focus on "Smooth Sailing Through Communication Channels," understanding that clear and consistent communication is crucial for successful partnerships.
- Establish effective communication protocols, provide regular updates, and ensure clients are informed throughout the partnership.
  Smooth Sailing Through Communication Channels ensures that the organization sails with a commitment to transparent and open communication, fostering trust and understanding. Like a captain ensuring smooth communication for a comfortable journey, your leadership maintains clear channels with clients.

Navigating Storms Together: Conflict Resolution in Client Relationships:
- Navigating storms together as a metaphor for conflict resolution in client relationships. Leaders prioritize "Navigating Storms Together: Conflict Resolution in Client

Relationships," recognizing that challenges may arise and need to be addressed promptly.

- Develop effective conflict resolution strategies, actively listen to client concerns, and collaborate on solutions. Navigating Storms Together ensures that the organization sails with resilience, addressing challenges and strengthening client relationships through effective conflict resolution. Similar to a captain navigating storms for passenger safety, your leadership resolves conflicts to ensure smooth client relationships.

Feedback and customer service excellence.

Pioneers with the Captain Sailor Attitude get it the significance of directing their organizations towards client benefit fabulousness, much like a captain guaranteeing travelers have an exceptional voyage. This analogical direct investigates how grasping client criticism and benefit fabulousness makes positive waves inside the organizational scene.

The Lighthouse of Customer Feedback:
- Customer feedback as the guiding lighthouse in the organizational seas. Leaders focus on "The Lighthouse of Customer Feedback," understanding that customer insights illuminate the path to service excellence.
- Establish a robust feedback system, actively solicit customer opinions, and use feedback as a beacon to improve products, services, and experiences. The Lighthouse of Customer Feedback ensures that the organization sails with clarity and direction provided by customer insights. Like a captain relying on a lighthouse for safe navigation, your leadership utilizes customer feedback as a guiding light for service excellence.

Listening to the Customer's Wind: Understanding Needs and Expectations:
- Listening to the customer's wind for understanding their needs and expectations. Leaders prioritize "Listening to the Customer's Wind," recognizing the importance of actively engaging with customers to grasp their preferences.
- Foster open communication channels, conduct regular surveys, and analyze customer behavior to understand their expectations. Listening to the Customer's Wind ensures that the organization sails with a clear understanding of customer needs, adjusting its course accordingly. Similar to a captain adjusting sails based on wind direction, your leadership adapts strategies based on customer expectations.

The Anchor of Service Excellence:
- Service excellence as the anchoring force for organizational success. Leaders focus on "The Anchor of Service Excellence," understanding that exceptional service holds the organization steady in turbulent waters.
- Establish service standards, train employees in service excellence, and consistently deliver exceptional customer experiences.
  The Anchor of Service Excellence ensures that the organization sails with a firm foundation of outstanding service. Like a captain relying on a sturdy anchor for stability, your leadership grounds the organization in service excellence.

Charting Courses with Customer Input: Collaborative Decision-Making:
- Collaborative decision-making as charting courses with customer input. Leaders prioritize "Charting Courses with Customer Input," recognizing the value of involving customers in decision-making processes.
- Seek customer opinions on strategic decisions, involve them in product development, and consider their input in shaping the organizational roadmap. Charting Courses with Customer Input ensures that the organization sails with a course guided by customer perspectives. Similar to a captain seeking input from passengers on the ship's course, your leadership values customer input in decision-making.

Chapter 25

Embarking on Innovation
Fostering a culture of innovation.

Within the tremendous ocean of viable administration, pioneers with the Captain Sailor Attitude recognize the significance of directing their organizations towards a culture of advancement. Much like a captain exploring unfamiliar waters, this analogical direct investigates how cultivating a culture of advancement makes positive waves inside the organizational scene.

The Compass of Creative Thinking:
- Creative thinking as the guiding compass in the organizational seas. Leaders focus on "The Compass of Creative Thinking," understanding that innovation is driven by a mindset that embraces imaginative solutions.
- Encourage brainstorming sessions, create spaces for free thinking, and celebrate creative ideas. The Compass of Creative Thinking ensures that the organization sails with a clear direction provided by innovative thoughts.
  Like a captain relying on a compass for navigation, your leadership utilizes creative thinking as a guiding force for innovation.

Setting Sail into Uncharted Territories: Encouraging Risk-Taking:
- Risk-taking as setting sail into uncharted territories. Leaders prioritize "Setting Sail into Uncharted Territories," recognizing that innovation often requires the courage to explore new and untested ideas.
- Foster a culture where calculated risks are encouraged, reward experimentation, and create an environment where failure is seen as a stepping stone to success. Setting Sail into Uncharted Territories ensures that the organization sails with the pioneering spirit needed for innovation. Similar to a captain exploring new routes for the ship's success, your leadership encourages risk-taking for innovative endeavors.

Navigating the Waves of Change: Adaptability and Flexibility:
- Adaptability and flexibility as navigating the waves of change. Leaders focus on "Navigating the Waves of Change," understanding that innovation often requires the ability to adapt to evolving circumstances.
- Emphasize agility in processes, encourage continuous learning, and instill a mindset that embraces change. Navigating the Waves of Change ensures that the organization sails with the flexibility needed to navigate innovation challenges. Like a captain adjusting to changing conditions at sea, your leadership adapts to the dynamic landscape of innovation.

Exploration Crew: Encouraging Cross-Functional Collaboration:
- Cross-functional collaboration as the exploration crew in the innovation journey. Leaders prioritize "Exploration Crew: Encouraging Cross-Functional Collaboration," recognizing that diverse perspectives enhance the innovation process.
- Break down silos, create interdisciplinary teams, and encourage collaboration across departments. Exploration Crew ensures that the organization sails with a crew that collaborates seamlessly for innovative outcomes. Similar to a captain relying on an exploration crew for diverse skills, your leadership fosters cross-functional collaboration for innovative success.

Innovative Navigation Tools: Providing Resources for Creativity:
- Resources for creativity as innovative navigation tools. Leaders focus on "Innovative Navigation Tools: Providing Resources for Creativity," understanding that innovation requires access to the right resources.
- Invest in training programs, provide access to cutting-edge technologies, and create an environment where employees have the tools they need to innovate. Innovative

Navigation Tools ensure that the organization sails with the resources required for a creative journey. Like a captain equipped with innovative navigation tools, your leadership provides resources for the journey of creativity.

Encouraging creativity and new ideas.

Leaders with the Captain Mariner Mindset understand the importance of fostering a culture that encourages creativity and new ideas. Much like a captain navigating uncharted waters, this analogical guide explores how embracing creativity creates positive waves within the organizational landscape.

The Canvas of Imagination:
- Imagination as the canvas on which the organizational journey is painted. Leaders focus on "The Canvas of Imagination," understanding that creativity begins with the ability to imagine possibilities.
- Create environments that stimulate imagination, encourage employees to dream big, and provide outlets for creative expression. The Canvas of Imagination ensures that the organization sails with a palette of ideas waiting to be explored. Like a captain who envisions new horizons, your leadership fosters a culture that values the limitless possibilities of imagination.

Navigating the Waters of Curiosity: Cultivating a Curious Crew:
- Curiosity as the compass guiding the organizational journey. Leaders prioritize "Navigating the Waters of Curiosity: Cultivating a Curious Crew," understanding that creativity flourishes when curiosity is embraced.
- Encourage a curious mindset, provide learning opportunities, and celebrate inquisitive thinking. Navigating the Waters of Curiosity ensures that the organization sails with a crew eager to explore new ideas. Similar to a captain relying on a compass for direction, your leadership cultivates a culture where curiosity is the guiding force for creative exploration.

Anchoring Innovation with Diverse Perspectives: Welcoming a Diverse Fleet:
- Diverse perspectives as the anchors securing innovative ideas. Leaders prioritize "Anchoring Innovation with Diverse Perspectives: Welcoming a Diverse Fleet," recognizing that creativity is enriched by a variety of viewpoints.
- Foster diversity and inclusion, actively seek input from varied backgrounds, and create spaces for open dialogue. Anchoring Innovation with Diverse Perspectives ensures that the organization sails with a fleet of ideas anchored in diverse experiences.
Like a captain relying on anchors for stability, your leadership values the strength that diverse perspectives bring to creative endeavors.

Building Bridges with Collaborative Creativity: Unifying Creative Forces:
- Collaborative creativity as the bridges connecting individual ideas. Leaders prioritize "Building Bridges with Collaborative Creativity: Unifying Creative Forces," understanding that collective innovation often surpasses individual efforts.
- Facilitate collaborative projects, establish platforms for idea-sharing, and encourage cross-functional partnerships. Building Bridges with Collaborative Creativity ensures that the organization sails with bridges that connect and strengthen individual creative forces. Similar to a captain relying on bridges for efficient navigation, your leadership fosters an environment where collaborative creativity flourishes.

Risk-taking and experimentation.

In the realm of effective management, leaders with the Captain Mariner Mindset recognize that success often lies beyond the comfort of familiar shores. This analogical guide explores the importance of risk-taking and experimentation, drawing parallels between navigating unexplored waters and forging a path to organizational success.

The Navigator's Dilemma: Embracing Uncertainty:

- Uncertainty as the uncharted territory demanding exploration. Leaders focus on "The Navigator's Dilemma: Embracing Uncertainty," understanding that risk-taking is the compass guiding the organization through unexplored waters.
- Cultivate a mindset that embraces uncertainty, encourage calculated risks, and create an environment where failure is viewed as a stepping stone to success. The Navigator's Dilemma ensures that the organization sails with the courage to explore uncharted territories. Like a captain navigating through unknown waters, your leadership embraces the challenges posed by uncertainty.

Setting Sail into the Abyss: Calculated Risk-Taking:

- Calculated risk-taking as setting sail into the abyss. Leaders prioritize "Setting Sail into the Abyss: Calculated Risk-Taking," recognizing that successful navigation requires evaluating risks and making informed decisions.
- Develop a risk assessment framework, encourage teams to analyze potential outcomes, and foster an environment where calculated risks are rewarded. Setting Sail into the Abyss ensures that the organization sails with a strategic approach to risk, balancing the potential for reward against possible challenges. Similar to a captain navigating through unpredictable waters, your leadership guides the organization with a calculated approach to risk-taking.

Storms on the Horizon: Navigating Failure and Learning:

- Failure as the stormy weather on the journey. Leaders prioritize "Storms on the Horizon: Navigating Failure and Learning," understanding that setbacks are an inherent part of risk-taking and experimentation.
- Encourage a culture that views failure as a learning opportunity, facilitate post-mortem analyses after unsuccessful endeavors, and extract valuable lessons from setbacks. Storms on the Horizon ensures that the organization sails with resilience, learning from challenges encountered on the journey. Like a captain navigating through storms, your leadership guides the organization through adversity with the lessons learned from failures.

Hoisting the Flag of Innovation: Experimentation and Creativity:

- Experimentation as hoisting the flag of innovation. Leaders focus on "Hoisting the Flag of Innovation: Experimentation and Creativity," recognizing that experimentation is the sail that propels the ship of progress.
- Create spaces for controlled experimentation, reward creative solutions, and instill a mindset that encourages trying new approaches. Hoisting the Flag of Innovation ensures that the organization sails with the wind of creativity, exploring new ideas and methods. Similar to a captain flying the flag of innovation, your leadership signals to the organization that experimentation is a valued part of the journey.

Chapter **26**

The Power of Recognition
The impact of acknowledging accomplishments.

In the expanse of effective management, leaders with the Captain Mariner Mindset understand the profound impact of acknowledging accomplishments on the journey to success. This analogical guide explores the importance of recognizing and celebrating achievements, drawing parallels between the captain's acknowledgment of milestones and the positive waves it creates within the organizational seas.

Landmarks on the Horizon: Significance of Milestone Acknowledgment:
- Acknowledging accomplishments as spotting landmarks on the horizon. Leaders prioritize the "Significance of Milestone Acknowledgment," understanding that recognizing achievements acts as beacons guiding the organization towards its goals.
- Establish a system for tracking and acknowledging milestones, celebrate both small and significant achievements, and ensure that the entire crew is aware of the progress. Landmarks on the Horizon ensures that the organization sails with a sense of direction and purpose, propelled by the acknowledgment of accomplishments. Like a captain spotting key landmarks, your leadership highlights the progress made towards the organizational vision.

The Beacon of Motivation: Fueling Crew Enthusiasm:
- Acknowledgment as the beacon of motivation guiding the crew. Leaders focus on the "Fueling Crew Enthusiasm," recognizing that acknowledging accomplishments boosts morale and propels the team towards higher performance.
- Implement a recognition and rewards program, communicate the impact of each achievement on the broader goals, and ensure that acknowledgment is timely and sincere. The Beacon of Motivation ensures that the organization sails with a motivated crew, inspired to achieve greater heights. Similar to a captain using beacons to guide the crew, your leadership fuels enthusiasm by acknowledging the team's successes.

Ripples of Positivity: Creating a Culture of Recognition:
- Creating a culture of recognition as generating ripples of positivity. Leaders prioritize "Creating a Culture of Recognition," understanding that acknowledgment sets the tone for a positive and collaborative work environment.
- Integrate acknowledgment into the organizational culture, encourage peer-to-peer recognition, and celebrate diverse achievements to create a holistic positive impact. Ripples of Positivity ensure that the organization sails with an atmosphere where every accomplishment contributes to the overall positive culture. Like a captain creating ripples by acknowledging the efforts of each crew member, your leadership fosters a culture where everyone's contributions are valued.

Anchors of Retention: Acknowledgment and Employee Engagement:
- Employee engagement as the anchors of retention. Leaders focus on "Acknowledgment and Employee Engagement," recognizing that acknowledging accomplishments strengthens the bonds between the crew and the organization.
- Implement engagement surveys, tailor acknowledgment to individual preferences, and incorporate acknowledgment into performance evaluations. Anchors of Retention ensure that the organization sails with a committed and engaged crew, reducing turnover and retaining valuable talent. Like a captain securing anchors for stability, your leadership uses acknowledgment to anchor employees to the organization.

Sailing through Storms: Acknowledgment in Challenging Times:
- Acknowledgment in challenging times as a guiding light through storms. Leaders prioritize "Acknowledgment in Challenging Times," understanding that recognizing accomplishments during difficulties boosts resilience and team cohesion.
- Acknowledge efforts during challenging projects, provide support and recognition during tough times, and celebrate the team's resilience. Sailing through Storms ensures that the organization sails through challenges with the guiding light of acknowledgment. Similar to a captain navigating through storms, your leadership uses acknowledgment as a source of inspiration and strength during difficult periods.

Public vs. private recognition.
Pioneers with the Captain Sailor Attitude get it the significance of recognizing achievements. Much like a beacon directing ships through stormy waters, this analogical direct investigates the affect of recognizing accomplishments and the nuanced approach of open versus private affirmation.

Navigating the Seas of Recognition: The Essence of Acknowledgment:
- Recognition as the guiding light in the vast seas of teamwork. Leaders focus on "Navigating the Seas of Recognition: The Essence of Acknowledgment," understanding that acknowledgment is the beacon that illuminates the path to success.
- Regularly acknowledge individual and team accomplishments, emphasizing the positive impact on the organization. Navigating the Seas of Recognition ensures that the organization sails with a sense of purpose and appreciation. Like a captain relying on a guiding light, your leadership shines a spotlight on the importance of acknowledgment in the journey.

Public Praise: Hoisting the Flag for All to See:
- Public praise as hoisting the flag of achievement. Leaders prioritize "Public Praise: Hoisting the Flag for All to See," recognizing that showcasing accomplishments publicly fosters a sense of pride and motivation.
- Celebrate achievements in team meetings, through company-wide announcements, or on public platforms. Public Praise ensures that the organization sails with a flag of success visible to all. Similar to a captain hoisting a flag for all to see, your leadership publicly acknowledges accomplishments, instilling a sense of shared achievement.

Private Commendations: The Personal Touch of Appreciation:
- Private commendations as the personal messages of appreciation. Leaders focus on "Private Commendations: The Personal Touch of Appreciation," understanding that individualized acknowledgment in private reinforces a strong sense of value.
- Send personalized messages, have one-on-one conversations, or use private channels to express appreciation for individual efforts. Private Commendations ensure that the organization sails with a personalized touch of gratitude.
  Like a captain conveying appreciation privately, your leadership recognizes the unique contributions of team members.

Casting Light on Team Success: Acknowledging Collective Achievements:
- Acknowledging collective achievements as casting light on the success of the entire crew. Leaders prioritize "Casting Light on Team Success: Acknowledging Collective Achievements," understanding that group acknowledgment reinforces a sense of unity.
- Celebrate team milestones, share success stories, and highlight group achievements in team settings. Casting Light on Team Success ensures that the organization sails with a collective spirit of accomplishment. Similar to a captain casting light on the success of the entire crew, your leadership recognizes and celebrates the achievements of the team as a whole.

When and how to recognize effectively.

In the realm of effective management, leaders with the Captain Mariner Mindset understand the crucial role of recognizing accomplishments in steering their teams towards success. This analogical guide explores the impact of acknowledging accomplishments, drawing parallels between a captain acknowledging the achievements of their crew and a leader fostering positive waves of motivation within the organizational waters.

The Lighthouse of Recognition: Illuminating the Path to Success:

- Recognition as the lighthouse guiding the organizational ship. Leaders prioritize "The Lighthouse of Recognition: Illuminating the Path to Success," understanding that acknowledging accomplishments is the beacon that guides teams through the challenges of the professional sea.
- Establish a culture of regular and sincere recognition, illuminating the path to success with moments of acknowledgment. The Lighthouse of Recognition ensures that the organization sails with a constant source of guidance, boosting morale and motivation. Like a captain relying on a lighthouse for safe navigation, your leadership provides a consistent source of encouragement.

Sails of Motivation: Boosting Morale through Recognition:

- Recognition as the wind filling the sails of motivation. Leaders prioritize "Sails of Motivation: Boosting Morale through Recognition," recognizing that acknowledging accomplishments is the wind that propels the team towards higher levels of performance.
- Implement a system of timely and specific recognition to provide the motivational wind needed for individual and collective success. Sails of Motivation ensures that the organization sails with a constant gust of positive energy, driving the team forward. Similar to a captain using the wind to propel the ship, your leadership harnesses the power of recognition for sustained motivation.

Harmony in the Crew: Fostering a Culture of Appreciation:

- Appreciation as the glue that binds the crew together. Leaders prioritize "Harmony in the Crew: Fostering a Culture of Appreciation," understanding that acknowledging accomplishments fosters a sense of unity and camaraderie.
- Encourage peer-to-peer recognition, celebrate team achievements, and weave a culture where appreciation becomes an integral part of the work environment. Harmony in the Crew ensures that the organization sails with a united crew, strengthened by the bonds of appreciation. Like a captain fostering camaraderie among the crew, your leadership builds a harmonious work culture.

The Navigator's Log: Documenting and Commemorating Achievements:

- Recognition as entries in the navigator's log. Leaders prioritize "The Navigator's Log: Documenting and Commemorating Achievements," understanding that acknowledging accomplishments is a way of preserving and commemorating the journey.
- Keep a record of individual and team accomplishments, celebrate milestones, and use the navigator's log as a tool for future motivation. The Navigator's Log ensures that the organization sails with a documented history of success, serving as a source of inspiration. Like a captain maintaining a log of the ship's journey, your leadership documents and commemorates achievements for continuous motivation.

Chapter **27**

Tides of Change: Managing Transitions
Leading organizational change.

In the vast ocean of organizational dynamics, leaders with the Captain Mariner Mindset understand that change is not merely a shift in direction but a journey to new horizons. This analogical guide explores the art of leading organizational change, drawing parallels between a captain guiding their ship through turbulent waters and a leader steering their team towards transformative success.

Charting a New Course: Visionary Leadership in Change Management:
- Visionary leadership as charting a new course. Leaders prioritize "Charting a New Course: Visionary Leadership in Change Management," recognizing that a clear vision is the compass that guides the organization through turbulent seas of change.
- Define a compelling vision for change, communicate it effectively to the team, and inspire commitment towards the shared destination. Charting a New Course ensures that the organization sails towards new horizons with clarity and purpose.
  Like a captain charting a course through uncharted waters, your leadership provides direction and inspiration during times of change.

Setting Sail with Stakeholder Engagement: Navigating Change Through Collaboration:
- Stakeholder engagement as setting sail with crew collaboration. Leaders prioritize "Setting Sail with Stakeholder Engagement: Navigating Change Through Collaboration," understanding that successful change requires the collective effort of all involved.
- Involve stakeholders in the change process, solicit their input and feedback, and foster a collaborative environment where everyone feels valued and heard. Setting Sail with Stakeholder Engagement ensures that the organization sails towards change with the wind of collective support. Similar to a captain relying on the expertise and collaboration of the crew, your leadership leverages stakeholder engagement for successful change navigation.

Navigating Choppy Waters: Anticipating and Managing Resistance:
- Managing resistance as navigating choppy waters.
  Leaders prioritize "Navigating Choppy Waters: Anticipating and Managing Resistance," understanding that resistance is a natural part of the change process.
- Anticipate potential sources of resistance, address concerns proactively, and provide support and resources to help individuals navigate through uncertainty. Navigating Choppy Waters ensures that the organization sails through resistance with resilience and adaptability. Like a captain steering through rough seas, your leadership guides the organization through periods of resistance with steadfast resolve.

Adjusting the Sails: Agile Adaptation in Change Management:
- Agile adaptation as adjusting the sails to changing winds. Leaders prioritize "Adjusting the Sails: Agile Adaptation in Change Management," recognizing that flexibility is essential when navigating the unpredictable currents of change.
- Embrace an agile mindset, be willing to pivot strategies based on feedback and emerging challenges, and encourage experimentation and learning throughout the change process. Adjusting the Sails ensures that the organization sails towards change with adaptability and responsiveness.
  Similar to a captain adjusting sails to catch the shifting winds, your leadership adapts strategies to navigate changing circumstances.

Celebrating Milestones: Anchoring Change with Positive Reinforcement:
- Celebrating milestones as anchoring change with positive reinforcement. Leaders prioritize "Celebrating Milestones: Anchoring Change with Positive Reinforcement,"

understanding that acknowledging progress reinforces commitment to the change journey.

- Recognize and celebrate milestones along the change journey, reinforcing the achievements and energizing the team for the remaining voyage. Celebrating Milestones ensures that the organization sails towards change with renewed motivation and enthusiasm. Like a captain anchoring at significant milestones to acknowledge progress, your leadership celebrates achievements to sustain momentum during change.

Breaking resistance to change.

Just as a skilled captain navigates through challenging waters, effective leaders with the Captain Mariner Mindset understand the importance of breaking resistance to change. In this analogical guide, we explore strategies for overcoming resistance to change by drawing parallels between a captain breaking through turbulent seas and a leader navigating organizational shifts.

Reading the Winds of Discontent: Understanding the Roots of Resistance:

- Understanding resistance as reading the winds of discontent. Leaders prioritize "Reading the Winds of Discontent: Understanding the Roots of Resistance," recognizing that to overcome resistance, one must first understand its origins.
- Engage in open communication, actively listen to concerns, and conduct assessments to identify the underlying factors contributing to resistance. Reading the Winds of Discontent ensures that the organization sails towards change with a comprehensive understanding of the sources of resistance.
  Like a captain assessing wind patterns for a smooth course, your leadership identifies the factors influencing resistance.

Casting the Visionary Net: Communicating a Compelling Future State:

- Communicating a compelling future state as casting the visionary net. Leaders prioritize "Casting the Visionary Net: Communicating a Compelling Future State," understanding that a clear vision helps in capturing the hearts and minds of the team.
- Articulate a compelling vision for the future, aligning it with the organization's values and demonstrating the positive outcomes of the proposed changes. Casting the Visionary Net ensures that the organization sails towards change with a shared and inspiring destination. Similar to a captain casting a net for a bountiful catch, your leadership casts a compelling vision to capture the commitment of the team.

Sailing Against the Wind: Leveraging Leadership Influence:

- Leveraging leadership influence as sailing against the wind. Leaders prioritize "Sailing Against the Wind: Leveraging Leadership Influence," understanding that sometimes overcoming resistance requires using the force of leadership.
- Utilize leadership influence to guide the team through change, reinforcing the benefits and emphasizing the collective strength gained by moving in the new direction. Sailing Against the Wind ensures that the organization sails towards change with the force of leadership propelling it forward. Like a captain steering against the wind, your leadership uses influence to navigate through resistance.

Flexible Navigation: Adapting Strategies to the Terrain of Resistance:

- Adapting strategies to the terrain of resistance as flexible navigation. Leaders prioritize "Flexible Navigation: Adapting Strategies to the Terrain of Resistance," understanding that rigid approaches may not always be effective.
- Adjust change strategies based on feedback, addressing specific concerns, and customizing communication to resonate with different team members. Flexible Navigation ensures that the organization sails towards change with adaptable and effective strategies. Similar to a captain adjusting the course based on changing conditions, your leadership adapts strategies to navigate diverse forms of resistance.

Guiding employees through transitions.

Navigating transitions within an organization can be likened to guiding a ship through ever-changing waters. Leaders with the Captain Mariner Mindset understand the significance of guiding employees through transitions smoothly. In this analogical guide, we explore strategies for effective leadership during periods of change, drawing parallels between a captain guiding a ship through dynamic seas and a leader steering their team through transitions.

Plotting the Course: Creating a Clear Transition Map:

- Creating a clear transition map as plotting the course. Leaders prioritize "Plotting the Course: Creating a Clear Transition Map," recognizing that a well-defined plan is essential for guiding employees through change.
- Develop a detailed transition plan that outlines the steps, timelines, and goals of the change process. Ensure clear communication to the team about the journey ahead. Plotting the Course ensures that the organization sails through transitions with a roadmap for success. Like a captain charting a course through unknown waters, your leadership provides a clear map for the team during transitions.

Setting the Compass: Aligning Team Goals with Organizational Objectives:

- Aligning team goals with organizational objectives as setting the compass. Leaders prioritize "Setting the Compass: Aligning Team Goals with Organizational Objectives," understanding that a unified direction is crucial for successful transitions.
- Ensure that individual and team goals align with the overarching objectives of the organization during the transition. Communicate the shared purpose and destination to foster a sense of unity. Setting the Compass ensures that the organization sails through transitions with coordinated efforts. Similar to a captain aligning the ship's compass with the destination, your leadership aligns team goals with organizational objectives.

Navigating the Waters: Providing Clear Communication and Support:

- Providing clear communication and support as navigating the waters. Leaders prioritize "Navigating the Waters: Providing Clear Communication and Support," recognizing that effective communication is the wind in the sails of successful transitions.
- Communicate openly and transparently about the changes, addressing concerns and providing support to alleviate uncertainties. Navigating the Waters ensures that the organization sails through transitions with clarity and a supportive environment. Like a captain navigating through complex waters, your leadership guides the team through changes with clear communication and unwavering support.

Fostering a Collaborative Crew: Encouraging Team Cohesion:

- Encouraging team cohesion as fostering a collaborative crew. Leaders prioritize "Fostering a Collaborative Crew: Encouraging Team Cohesion," understanding that a united team is better equipped to navigate transitions.
- Promote a collaborative and supportive team culture, encouraging open dialogue and collaboration. Foster a sense of camaraderie to help the team weather the challenges of transitions together. Fostering a Collaborative Crew ensures that the organization sails through transitions with a cohesive and resilient team. Similar to a captain fostering unity among the crew, your leadership encourages team cohesion during transitions.

Chapter **28**

Assembling a Fleet
Scaling management practices for growth.

Scaling management practices for growth can be likened to expanding a ship's operations to encompass larger and more challenging waters. Leaders with the Captain Mariner Mindset recognize the importance of adapting management approaches to sustain and navigate growth effectively. In this analogical guide, we explore strategies for scaling management practices, drawing parallels between a captain expanding the ship's reach and a leader extending their management capabilities for organizational growth.

Charting the Expansion: Developing a Strategic Growth Plan:
- Developing a strategic growth plan as charting the expansion. Leaders prioritize "Charting the Expansion: Developing a Strategic Growth Plan," understanding the necessity of a well-thought-out strategy when scaling management practices.
- Develop a comprehensive growth plan that outlines goals, identifies potential challenges, and establishes a roadmap for scaling management practices.
Consider the organization's current state and future objectives when charting the expansion. Just as a captain plans the course for an extended journey, your leadership plans the strategic growth path for the organization.

Expanding Crew Capabilities: Investing in Leadership Development:
- Investing in leadership development as expanding crew capabilities. Leaders prioritize "Expanding Crew Capabilities: Investing in Leadership Development," recognizing that a skilled and adaptable team is essential for navigating growth.
- Invest in leadership training and development programs to enhance the skills of managers and leaders within the organization. Foster a culture of continuous learning to ensure that the crew (team) is equipped to handle the challenges of growth. Expanding Crew Capabilities ensures that the organization sails towards growth with a capable and well-prepared team. Like a captain investing in crew training for new challenges, your leadership invests in developing the capabilities of the management team.

Navigating New Waters: Adapting Leadership Styles to Growth Phases:
- Adapting leadership styles to growth phases as navigating new waters. Leaders prioritize "Navigating New Waters: Adapting Leadership Styles to Growth Phases," understanding that different growth stages require flexible leadership approaches.
- Recognize the distinct needs of the organization during different growth phases and adapt leadership styles accordingly. Be agile in adjusting management practices to align with the evolving requirements of the team and the business. Navigating New Waters ensures that the organization sails through growth with leadership that can navigate diverse challenges. Similar to a captain adjusting to different sea conditions, your leadership adapts to varying growth phases.

Streamlining Operations: Enhancing Efficiency for Scalability:
- Enhancing efficiency for scalability as streamlining operations. Leaders prioritize "Streamlining Operations: Enhancing Efficiency for Scalability," understanding that streamlined processes are critical for managing growth effectively.
- Evaluate and optimize operational processes to ensure they can scale seamlessly with the growth of the organization. Implement technologies and systems that enhance efficiency and support scalability. Streamlining Operations ensures that the organization sails towards growth with optimized and scalable management practices. Like a captain streamlining ship operations for increased capacity, your leadership optimizes organizational processes for scalability.

Crew Alignment with Organizational Vision: Communicating Growth Objectives:
- Communicating growth objectives as crew alignment with organizational vision. Leaders prioritize "Crew Alignment with Organizational Vision: Communicating Growth Objectives," recognizing that a united team is crucial for achieving growth goals.
- Communicate transparently about growth objectives, ensuring that the entire team understands and aligns with the organizational vision. Foster a shared sense of purpose to inspire commitment and collaboration. Crew Alignment with Organizational Vision ensures that the organization sails through growth with a cohesive and aligned team.

Coordination among different teams and departments.

Achieving coordination among different teams and departments is comparable to ensuring seamless collaboration between various components of a ship's crew. Leaders with the Captain Mariner Mindset understand the significance of orchestrating harmony among diverse teams to steer the organization towards success. In this analogical guide, we explore strategies for effective coordination, drawing parallels between a captain synchronizing crew activities and a leader facilitating collaboration across teams and departments.

Navigation by Consensus: Establishing Collective Goals and Objectives:
- Establishing collective goals and objectives as navigation by consensus. Leaders prioritize "Navigation by Consensus: Establishing Collective Goals and Objectives," recognizing that aligning teams with shared goals is essential for successful coordination.
- Engage teams in the process of defining collective goals and objectives that align with the overarching mission of the organization.
  Facilitate discussions to reach a consensus, fostering a sense of ownership and commitment. Navigation by Consensus ensures that the organization sails through collaboration with teams working towards a common destination. Like a captain steering the ship by consensus, your leadership guides teams toward shared goals.

Commanding a Unified Fleet: Promoting Cross-Functional Collaboration:
- Promoting cross-functional collaboration as commanding a unified fleet. Leaders prioritize "Commanding a Unified Fleet: Promoting Cross-Functional Collaboration," understanding that collaboration across different departments is crucial for synchronized efforts.
- Encourage cross-functional collaboration by breaking down silos and promoting open communication between departments. Create platforms for teams to share insights, expertise, and resources, fostering a unified approach. Commanding a Unified Fleet ensures that the organization sails through coordination with departments working together seamlessly. Similar to a captain leading a unified fleet, your leadership promotes collaboration across diverse departments.

Harmonizing Team Dynamics: Cultivating Interdepartmental Relationships:
- Cultivating interdepartmental relationships as harmonizing team dynamics. Leaders prioritize "Harmonizing Team Dynamics: Cultivating Interdepartmental Relationships," understanding that strong relationships between teams are the bedrock of effective coordination.
- Foster a culture of collaboration by organizing cross-departmental events, workshops, or team-building activities. Facilitate opportunities for teams to understand each other's functions, fostering mutual respect and understanding. Harmonizing Team Dynamics ensures that the organization sails through coordination with interdepartmental relationships that are harmonious and supportive. Like a captain ensuring harmony among the crew, your leadership cultivates positive relationships between departments.

Multi-team projects and inter-departmental collaboration.

Managing multi-team projects and fostering inter-departmental collaboration can be compared to steering a ship through complex waters with multiple currents. Leaders with the Captain Mariner Mindset understand the importance of cohesive teamwork and coordination to ensure the success of such endeavors. In this analogical guide, we explore strategies for effective management in multi-team projects, drawing parallels between a captain navigating diverse waters and a leader orchestrating collaboration across various departments.

Charting the Collaborative Course: Creating a Project Blueprint:

- Creating a project blueprint as charting the collaborative course. Leaders prioritize "Charting the Collaborative Course: Creating a Project Blueprint," recognizing that a well-defined plan is essential for steering multi-team projects.
- Develop a detailed project plan that outlines roles, responsibilities, timelines, and milestones. Ensure that all teams involved have a clear understanding of the collaborative journey.

  Charting the Collaborative Course ensures that the project sails smoothly through the complexities of multi-team collaboration. Like a captain charting a course through diverse waters, your leadership charts the collaborative course for the project.

Harmonizing Diverse Crews: Fostering a Unified Team Spirit:

- Fostering a unified team spirit as harmonizing diverse crews. Leaders prioritize "Harmonizing Diverse Crews: Fostering a Unified Team Spirit," understanding that a cohesive and collaborative team spirit is crucial for successful multi-team projects.
- Promote a culture of unity and cooperation among teams, fostering open communication and shared goals. Recognize and celebrate achievements across departments to build a sense of camaraderie. Harmonizing Diverse Crews ensures that the project sails through challenges with a unified and motivated team. Similar to a captain fostering unity among diverse crew members, your leadership unifies teams for successful multi-team projects.

Navigating Cross-Functional Waters: Facilitating Inter-Departmental Communication:

- Facilitating inter-departmental communication as navigating cross-functional waters. Leaders prioritize "Navigating Cross-Functional Waters: Facilitating Inter-Departmental Communication," recognizing that effective communication is essential for the smooth flow of information across teams.
- Establish clear channels for communication between departments, fostering an environment where information can flow seamlessly. Encourage regular updates, feedback sessions, and collaborative meetings to enhance cross-functional communication. Navigating Cross-Functional Waters ensures that the project sails through complexities with effective communication between departments. Like a captain navigating through cross-functional waters, your leadership facilitates communication among diverse teams.

Chapter **29**

The Mentorship Rig
The role of mentorship in leadership development.

The role of mentorship in leadership development is akin to having an experienced navigator guiding a ship through challenging waters. Leaders with the Captain Mariner Mindset understand the profound impact mentorship can have on shaping effective leadership. In this analogical guide, we delve into the strategies of mentorship, drawing parallels between a captain guiding a ship and a mentor fostering leadership development.

Casting the Mentorship Net: Identifying Potential Mentors and Mentees:
- Identifying potential mentors and mentees as casting the mentorship net. Leaders prioritize "Casting the Mentorship Net: Identifying Potential Mentors and Mentees," understanding that a successful mentorship program begins with the right connections.
- Encourage the identification and pairing of potential mentors and mentees within the organization. Consider individual strengths, skills, and areas for development when casting the mentorship net.

  This ensures that the mentorship program is well-aligned with the needs and aspirations of both mentors and mentees. Just as a captain selects an experienced navigator for specific challenges, your leadership casts the mentorship net to foster tailored guidance.

Setting Sail on the Mentorship Journey: Structuring Mentorship Programs:
- Structuring mentorship programs as setting sail on the mentorship journey. Leaders prioritize "Setting Sail on the Mentorship Journey: Structuring Mentorship Programs," recognizing the importance of a well-organized and goal-oriented mentorship initiative.
- Develop a structured mentorship program that includes clear objectives, defined timelines, and measurable goals. Provide resources and support for mentors and mentees to navigate the mentorship journey effectively. Structuring Mentorship Programs ensures that the organization sails smoothly through leadership development with a well-planned and goal-driven mentorship initiative. Like a captain planning a journey with a set course, your leadership structures mentorship programs for a purposeful leadership development journey.

Navigating the Leadership Seas: Personalized Guidance and Support:
- Personalized guidance and support as navigating the leadership seas. Leaders prioritize "Navigating the Leadership Seas: Personalized Guidance and Support," understanding that effective mentorship involves tailored assistance for individual growth.
- Encourage mentors to provide personalized guidance and support to mentees, addressing specific challenges and fostering individual development. Ensure that the mentorship relationship is based on open communication and mutual understanding. Navigating the Leadership Seas ensures that leaders receive the personalized guidance needed for successful leadership development. Similar to a captain guiding the ship through unique navigational challenges, your leadership provides tailored support through mentorship.

Calibrating the Compass: Regular Check-ins and Feedback:
- Regular check-ins and feedback as calibrating the compass. Leaders prioritize "Calibrating the Compass: Regular Check-ins and Feedback," recognizing that ongoing assessment and adjustment are crucial for mentorship success.
- Establish a system of regular check-ins and feedback sessions between mentors and mentees. Create a supportive environment for honest discussions about progress,

challenges, and areas for improvement. Calibrating the Compass ensures that the mentorship journey stays on course, with continuous adjustments to meet evolving needs. Like a captain regularly calibrating the ship's compass, your leadership ensures the mentorship program stays aligned with individual and organizational objectives.

Navigational Skill Transfer: Knowledge and Experience Sharing:
- Knowledge and experience sharing as navigational skill transfer. Leaders prioritize "Navigational Skill Transfer: Knowledge and Experience Sharing," understanding that mentorship involves the transfer of valuable skills and insights.
- Encourage mentors to share their knowledge, experiences, and practical skills with mentees. Foster a culture of learning and mutual exchange within the mentorship relationship. Navigational Skill Transfer ensures that leadership capabilities are enriched through the transfer of valuable skills and experiences..

Setting up a mentorship program.

Setting up a mentorship program is comparable to preparing a ship for a successful voyage. Leaders with the Captain Mariner Mindset recognize the importance of a well-structured mentorship initiative in fostering effective management. In this analogical guide, we explore the strategies of setting up a mentorship program, drawing parallels between preparing a ship for a journey and establishing a program for leadership development.

Plotting the Course: Defining Clear Objectives for the Mentorship Program:
- Defining clear objectives for the mentorship program as plotting the course. Leaders prioritize "Plotting the Course: Defining Clear Objectives for the Mentorship Program," understanding that a successful mentorship journey begins with a well-defined path.
- Clearly articulate the objectives of the mentorship program, outlining the specific goals it aims to achieve. Ensure alignment with organizational objectives and the developmental needs of participants.
  Plotting the Course sets a clear direction for the mentorship program, just as a captain charts the course for a successful voyage.

Preparing the Crew: Identifying and Matching Mentors and Mentees:
- Identifying and matching mentors and mentees as preparing the crew. Leaders prioritize "Preparing the Crew: Identifying and Matching Mentors and Mentees," recognizing that success depends on assembling the right team.
- Conduct thorough assessments to identify potential mentors and mentees. Consider individual strengths, experiences, and areas for development when making mentor-mentee pairs. Preparing the Crew ensures that the mentorship program has a strong foundation, similar to a captain assembling a skilled and cohesive crew for a voyage.

Inspecting the Vessel: Creating a Supportive Program Structure:
- Creating a supportive program structure as inspecting the vessel. Leaders prioritize "Inspecting the Vessel: Creating a Supportive Program Structure," understanding the importance of a well-maintained and supportive structure.
- Develop a structured mentorship program with defined timelines, milestones, and resources. Ensure that mentors and mentees have the necessary support to navigate the program successfully. Inspecting the Vessel creates a solid foundation for the mentorship initiative, akin to a captain ensuring the ship is in optimal condition for the journey.

Navigating the Seas: Providing Training and Resources for Mentors:
- Providing training and resources for mentors as navigating the seas. Leaders prioritize "Navigating the Seas: Providing Training and Resources for Mentors," recognizing that effective mentors need the right skills and tools.
- Offer training sessions and resources to mentors, equipping them with the necessary skills to guide and support their mentees effectively. Navigating the Seas ensures that

mentors are well-prepared for their role, similar to a captain being trained to navigate challenging waters.

Qualities of a good mentor and mentee.
In the realm of effective management, a successful mentorship relationship is akin to having a skilled navigator guiding a ship through dynamic waters. Leaders with the Captain Mariner Mindset understand the pivotal role that qualities of a good mentor and mentee play in steering the course of leadership development. In this analogical guide, we explore the essential qualities of both mentors and mentees, drawing parallels between the traits needed for a successful mentorship and the qualities crucial for navigating the seas.

Captain's Wisdom: Qualities of a Good Mentor:
- Qualities of a good mentor as possessing the wisdom of a seasoned captain. Leaders prioritize "Captain's Wisdom: Qualities of a Good Mentor," understanding that effective mentors are akin to experienced navigators.
- A good mentor possesses industry experience, a deep understanding of organizational dynamics, and the ability to provide insightful guidance. They excel in communication, empathy, and the willingness to share their wisdom.
Captain's Wisdom ensures that mentors navigate the mentorship waters with expertise, much like a seasoned captain guiding a ship through intricate routes.

Navigator's Eagerness: Qualities of a Good Mentee:
- Qualities of a good mentee as embodying the eagerness of a dedicated navigator. Leaders prioritize "Navigator's Eagerness: Qualities of a Good Mentee," recognizing that successful mentees approach the mentorship journey with a thirst for knowledge.
- A good mentee is eager to learn, open to feedback, and proactive in seeking guidance. They demonstrate initiative, accountability, and a genuine interest in professional growth. Navigator's Eagerness ensures that mentees actively participate in their development, much like a dedicated navigator eager to explore new horizons.

Compassionate Leadership: Empathy in Mentorship:
- Empathy in mentorship as embodying compassionate leadership. Leaders prioritize "Compassionate Leadership: Empathy in Mentorship," understanding that effective mentorship requires a genuine connection.
- A good mentor empathizes with the challenges faced by their mentee, offering support and encouragement. They foster a trusting relationship, creating a safe space for mentees to share concerns and seek guidance. Compassionate Leadership ensures that mentorship is built on a foundation of understanding and empathy, much like a captain leading with compassion in challenging seas.

Navigator's Initiative: Proactiveness in Mentees:
- Proactiveness in mentees as embodying the initiative of a skilled navigator. Leaders prioritize "Navigator's Initiative: Proactiveness in Mentees," recognizing the importance of mentees taking an active role in their development.
- A good mentee takes initiative, identifies areas for improvement, and actively seeks opportunities for growth. They demonstrate a proactive approach to their professional journey. Navigator's Initiative ensures that mentees actively contribute to the mentorship relationship, similar to a skilled navigator taking initiative in navigating the ship through varying conditions.

Chapter **30**

Celebrating Success
The importance of celebrating milestones.

In the vast sea of effective management, celebrating milestones is comparable to marking significant achievements on a successful voyage. Leaders with the Captain Mariner Mindset understand the profound impact of recognizing and celebrating accomplishments. In this analogical guide, we explore the importance of celebrating milestones, drawing parallels between the joyous moments of a successful sea journey and the positive waves generated by acknowledging and honoring achievements in the workplace.

Navigational Beacons: Significance of Celebrating Milestones:
- Significance of celebrating milestones as akin to navigational beacons guiding the way. Leaders prioritize the "Navigational Beacons: Significance of Celebrating Milestones," understanding that these moments serve as guiding lights in the journey of effective management.
- Celebrating milestones acknowledges and highlights achievements, providing a sense of direction and purpose for the team.
  Like navigational beacons guiding a ship through the seas, recognizing milestones helps steer the organization toward its goals.

Crew's Joyous Cheers: Boosting Morale through Celebrations:
- Boosting morale through celebrations as comparable to the joyous cheers of a satisfied crew. Leaders prioritize "Crew's Joyous Cheers: Boosting Morale through Celebrations," recognizing that celebrating achievements lifts the spirits of the team.
- Celebrating milestones fosters a positive and uplifting work environment. It boosts team morale, creating a sense of camaraderie and shared success. Just as the crew's joyous cheers echo across the ship, celebrations resonate throughout the workplace, energizing the team for future endeavors.

Anchors of Recognition: Building a Culture of Appreciation:
- Building a culture of appreciation as anchors of recognition. Leaders prioritize "Anchors of Recognition: Building a Culture of Appreciation," understanding that consistent acknowledgment is foundational to organizational success.
- Celebrating milestones establishes a culture where achievements are recognized and valued.
  Similar to anchors providing stability to a ship, regular recognition anchors a positive culture within the organization, reinforcing the importance of each team member's contributions.

Harvesting Positive Waves: Inspiring Continued Excellence:
- Inspiring continued excellence as harvesting positive waves. Leaders prioritize "Harvesting Positive Waves: Inspiring Continued Excellence," recognizing that celebrating milestones motivates the team to strive for ongoing success.
- Celebrating milestones serves as a source of inspiration, encouraging individuals and teams to pursue excellence. Just as harvesting positive waves ensures a bountiful journey, recognizing achievements inspires the continuous pursuit of excellence in the workplace.

Navigating the Future: Setting the Course for Future Success:
- Setting the course for future success as navigating the future. Leaders prioritize "Navigating the Future: Setting the Course for Future Success," understanding that celebrating milestones establishes a trajectory for ongoing achievement.

- Recognizing and celebrating milestones not only honors past accomplishments but also sets the course for future success. Like plotting a navigational course for upcoming voyages, celebrating achievements guides the organization toward new milestones and goals.

Organizing team events and celebrations.

In the vast expanse of effective management, organizing team events and celebrations is comparable to fostering a sense of unity and camaraderie on a well-sailed ship. Leaders with the Captain Mariner Mindset understand the significance of bonding moments and shared experiences. In this analogical guide, we explore the importance of organizing team events and celebrations, drawing parallels between the coordination of ship activities and the positive waves generated by team cohesion in the workplace.

Harbor of Unity: Significance of Team Events and Celebrations:
- Significance of team events and celebrations as the harbor of unity. Leaders prioritize the "Harbor of Unity: Significance of Team Events and Celebrations," recognizing that these occasions serve as anchor points for team cohesion.
- Team events and celebrations provide a harbor where team members can come together, fostering a sense of unity. Just as a harbor offers a secure and collective space for ships, these occasions create a collective atmosphere, strengthening the bonds among team members.

Synchronized Crew: Enhancing Team Coordination:
- Enhancing team coordination as having a synchronized crew on board. Leaders prioritize "Synchronized Crew: Enhancing Team Coordination," understanding that coordinated efforts lead to smoother operations.
- Team events and celebrations allow team members to synchronize and align their efforts outside the usual work context. Like a well-coordinated crew ensuring the smooth operation of a ship, these occasions enhance team coordination, creating a harmonious work environment.

Raising the Team Flag: Building a Collective Identity:
- Building a collective identity as raising the team flag. Leaders prioritize "Raising the Team Flag: Building a Collective Identity," recognizing the importance of a shared identity within the team.
- Team events and celebrations contribute to the development of a collective identity. Similar to raising a team flag that symbolizes unity, these occasions strengthen the sense of belonging and shared purpose among team members.

Anchoring Trust: Strengthening Team Bonds:
- Strengthening team bonds as anchoring trust.
  Leaders prioritize "Anchoring Trust: Strengthening Team Bonds," understanding that trust is fundamental to effective teamwork.
- Team events and celebrations provide opportunities for team members to connect on a personal level, building trust. Like anchors securing a ship in place, these occasions anchor trust within the team, fostering a supportive and collaborative work environment.

Navigational Breaks: Promoting Well-Deserved Rest:
- Promoting well-deserved rest as taking navigational breaks. Leaders prioritize "Navigational Breaks: Promoting Well-Deserved Rest," understanding the importance of rejuvenation for sustained performance.
- Team events and celebrations serve as navigational breaks, offering team members a chance to relax and recharge. Similar to the breaks a ship takes during a voyage, these occasions promote well-deserved rest, contributing to overall team well-being and productivity.

Recognizing individual and team contributions.

In the vast seas of effective management, recognizing individual and team contributions is akin to navigating with the Captain Mariner Mindset. In this analogical guide, we explore the importance of acknowledging the efforts of each crew member, drawing parallels between recognizing contributions in the workplace and the cohesive synergy required for smooth sailing.

Navigating with Precision: Significance of Recognizing Contributions:

- Significance of recognizing contributions as navigating with precision. Leaders prioritize the "Navigating with Precision: Significance of Recognizing Contributions," understanding that precise acknowledgment steers the team towards success.
- Acknowledging individual and team contributions ensures that everyone is recognized for their unique role in achieving organizational goals. Just as precise navigation is crucial for a successful voyage, recognizing contributions ensures the team is aligned and moving in the right direction.

Harmonious Symphony: Fostering Team Unity through Acknowledgment:

- Fostering team unity through acknowledgment is comparable to a harmonious symphony. Leaders prioritize "Harmonious Symphony: Fostering Team Unity through Acknowledgment," recognizing that acknowledgment is the melody that unites the team.
- Acknowledging individual and team contributions fosters a harmonious work environment. Like instruments in a symphony contributing to the overall melody, recognizing each team member's efforts creates a united and cooperative work culture.

Anchors of Appreciation: Building a Culture of Recognition:

- Building a culture of recognition as anchors of appreciation. Leaders prioritize "Anchors of Appreciation: Building a Culture of Recognition," understanding that consistent acknowledgment is foundational for organizational success.
- Recognizing contributions establishes a culture where every effort is valued. Similar to anchors providing stability to a ship, regular recognition anchors a positive culture within the organization, reinforcing the importance of each team member's contributions.

Cultivating Positive Waves: Motivating Ongoing Excellence:

- Motivating ongoing excellence as cultivating positive waves. Leaders prioritize "Cultivating Positive Waves: Motivating Ongoing Excellence," recognizing that acknowledgment serves as a motivator for continuous improvement.
- Acknowledging contributions serves as a source of inspiration, encouraging individuals and teams to pursue ongoing excellence. Just as cultivating positive waves ensures a positive journey, recognizing efforts motivates the team to consistently deliver their best.

Setting Sail with Gratitude: Expressing Thanks for a Collective Journey:

- Expressing thanks for a collective journey is setting sail with gratitude. Leaders prioritize "Setting Sail with Gratitude: Expressing Thanks for a Collective Journey," understanding that expressing gratitude is a powerful leadership tool.
- Acknowledging contributions is an expression of gratitude for the collective journey. Like setting sail with gratitude ensures a positive and thankful atmosphere, recognizing efforts fosters a culture where individuals feel valued and appreciated for their contributions.

Chapter **31**

Quality Overboard: Driving Excellence
Defining and measuring quality.

In the sea of effective management, defining and measuring quality is akin to navigating with the Captain Mariner Mindset. In this analogical guide, we explore the importance of setting the compass for excellence, drawing parallels between defining and measuring quality in the workplace and the precision required for smooth sailing.

Navigating Excellence: The Significance of Defining Quality:
- Significance of defining quality as navigating towards excellence. Leaders prioritize "Navigating Excellence: The Significance of Defining Quality," understanding that a clear definition of quality sets the course for success.
- Defining quality ensures a shared understanding of expectations and standards. Just as navigating towards excellence requires a clear course, defining quality establishes a framework for the team to consistently deliver high-performance results.

Harmony in Standards: Fostering Consistency through Definition:
- Fostering consistency through definition is comparable to achieving harmony in standards. Leaders prioritize "Harmony in Standards: Fostering Consistency through Definition," recognizing that a clear definition of quality creates a consistent and cohesive work environment.
- Defining quality sets a standard that harmonizes efforts across the team. Like achieving harmony in standards ensures a seamless journey, a clear definition of quality fosters consistency and coherence in the team's deliverables.

Anchors of Precision: Building a Culture of Quality Measurement:
- Building a culture of quality measurement as anchors of precision. Leaders prioritize "Anchors of Precision: Building a Culture of Quality Measurement," understanding that consistent measurement is foundational for organizational success.
- Measuring quality becomes an anchor, providing stability to the organization. Similar to anchors ensuring steadiness for a ship, consistent measurement of quality establishes a solid foundation for continuous improvement.

Cultivating Positive Waves: Motivating Continuous Improvement:
- Motivating continuous improvement as cultivating positive waves. Leaders prioritize "Cultivating Positive Waves: Motivating Continuous Improvement," recognizing that quality measurement serves as a motivator for ongoing excellence.
- Measuring quality becomes a source of inspiration, encouraging individuals and teams to pursue continuous improvement. Just as cultivating positive waves ensures a positive journey, measuring quality motivates the team to consistently enhance their performance.

Setting the Course with Metrics: Guiding the Team towards Success:
- Guiding the team towards success by setting the course with metrics. Leaders prioritize "Setting the Course with Metrics: Guiding the Team towards Success," understanding that metrics serve as a guiding compass for the organization.
- Measuring quality through metrics ensures the team is on the right course. Like setting the course with a guiding compass ensures a successful voyage, defining and measuring quality with metrics guides the team towards success.

Continuous quality improvement methods.

In the expansive sea of effective management, navigating through continuous quality improvement is akin to sailing with the Captain Mariner Mindset. In this analogical guide, we explore the significance of perpetually enhancing quality, drawing parallels between continuous quality improvement methods and the precise navigation required for smooth sailing.

Sailing the Waters of Refinement: The Essence of Continuous Quality Improvement:
- The essence of continuous quality improvement is akin to sailing the waters of refinement. Leaders prioritize "Sailing the Waters of Refinement: The Essence of Continuous Quality Improvement," understanding that ongoing enhancement is key to organizational success.
- Continuous quality improvement ensures the organization is in a perpetual state of refinement. Just as sailing through refined waters ensures a smooth voyage, adopting methods for continuous quality improvement guarantees a journey of perpetual enhancement.

Harmony in Evolution: Fostering Growth through Iterative Progress:
- Fostering growth through iterative progress is comparable to achieving harmony in evolution. Leaders prioritize "Harmony in Evolution: Fostering Growth through Iterative Progress," recognizing that consistent refinement leads to overall organizational evolution.
- Continuous quality improvement methods foster an environment of constant evolution. Like achieving harmony in evolution ensures a seamless journey, iterative progress in quality enhancement cultivates a culture of ongoing growth within the organization.

Anchors of Consistent Progress: Building a Culture of Continuous Improvement:
- Building a culture of continuous improvement is akin to securing anchors of consistent progress. Leaders prioritize "Anchors of Consistent Progress: Building a Culture of Continuous Improvement," understanding that a culture supporting continuous improvement serves as a foundation for success.
- Continuous quality improvement becomes an anchor for the organization's consistent progress.
  Similar to anchors providing stability to a ship, a culture of continuous improvement establishes a solid foundation for sustained success.

Cultivating Positive Waves: Motivating Teams towards Excellence:
- Motivating teams towards excellence through continuous quality improvement is comparable to cultivating positive waves. Leaders prioritize "Cultivating Positive Waves: Motivating Teams towards Excellence," recognizing that ongoing improvement serves as a powerful motivator for teams.
- Continuous quality improvement becomes a source of inspiration, encouraging teams to strive for excellence. Just as cultivating positive waves ensures a positive journey, motivating teams through continuous quality improvement methods guarantees a path toward excellence.

Role of management in quality assurance.

In the vast expanse of effective management, steering the ship of quality assurance requires the steadfast Captain Mariner Mindset. In this analogical guide, we explore the critical role of management in quality assurance, drawing parallels between the captain's responsibilities and the precision needed for smooth sailing in the realm of quality assurance.

Captain at the Helm: Leadership's Role in Defining Quality Standards:
- Leadership's role in defining quality standards is comparable to the captain at the helm setting the ship's course. Leaders prioritize "Captain at the Helm: Leadership's Role in Defining Quality Standards," understanding that a clear direction is crucial for quality assurance.
- Management, like a captain at the helm, must establish clear quality standards. Just as a captain charts the course for the ship's success, leadership sets the direction for quality assurance, ensuring a clear path for the team.

Navigating Uncharted Waters: Adapting Strategies to Ensure Quality:
- Adapting strategies to ensure quality is akin to a captain navigating uncharted waters. Leaders prioritize "Navigating Uncharted Waters: Adapting Strategies to Ensure Quality," recognizing the need for flexibility and innovation in quality assurance.
- Management, like a captain navigating unknown seas, must adapt strategies to ensure quality. Just as a captain adjusts to changing conditions, leadership adapts quality assurance strategies to tackle new challenges and uncertainties.

Anchors of Precision: Establishing Protocols for Quality Control:
- Establishing protocols for quality control is comparable to anchors of precision securing the ship. Leaders prioritize "Anchors of Precision: Establishing Protocols for Quality Control," understanding that stringent protocols ensure stability in quality assurance.
- Management serves as anchors of precision by establishing and enforcing protocols for quality control. Similar to anchors ensuring the ship's stability, protocols maintain the stability and consistency of quality in the realm of quality assurance.

Crew Training and Preparedness: Building a Quality-Centric Culture:
- Building a quality-centric culture through crew training is akin to preparing the ship's crew for excellence. Leaders prioritize "Crew Training and Preparedness: Building a Quality-Centric Culture," recognizing that a trained and prepared team is essential for quality assurance.
- Management ensures crew training and preparedness for quality-centric practices. Like a captain preparing the crew for the journey, leadership instills a culture of quality awareness and excellence among team members in the realm of quality assurance.

Cultivating Positive Waves: Motivating Teams for Quality Excellence:
- Motivating teams for quality excellence is comparable to cultivating positive waves. Leaders prioritize "Cultivating Positive Waves: Motivating Teams for Quality Excellence," understanding that motivation is key to achieving high standards in quality assurance.
- Management becomes the source of positive waves, motivating teams for quality excellence.

Chapter **32**

The Trade Winds: Networking and Partnerships
The importance of external relations.

In the maritime world of effective management, the Captain Mariner Mindset extends beyond the ship's deck, emphasizing the significance of external relations. This guide explores the parallels between managing external relationships and smooth sailing, illustrating how a captain's approach can be translated into effective management strategies for creating positive waves in external interactions.

Setting Sail in Uncharted Waters: Initiating and Nurturing Partnerships:
- Initiating and nurturing partnerships are akin to setting sail in uncharted waters. Leaders prioritize "Setting Sail in Uncharted Waters: Initiating and Nurturing Partnerships," understanding the need for exploration and relationship-building in external relations.
- Management, like a captain venturing into uncharted waters, must proactively initiate and nurture partnerships. By doing so, they expand the organization's horizons, fostering collaborations that contribute to its success.

Navigating Diplomatic Channels: Diplomacy in External Interactions:
- Diplomacy in external interactions is comparable to navigating diplomatic channels. Leaders prioritize "Navigating Diplomatic Channels: Diplomacy in External Interactions," recognizing that tact and diplomacy are essential when dealing with external stakeholders.
- Management, like a captain navigating diplomatic waters, must employ tact and diplomacy in external interactions. By doing so, they build positive relationships, resolve conflicts amicably, and ensure a smooth course in the seas of external engagements.

Weathering Storms: Crisis Management in External Relations:
- Crisis management in external relations is akin to weathering storms. Leaders prioritize "Weathering Storms: Crisis Management in External Relations," understanding the need to navigate challenges gracefully and maintain stability in turbulent times.
- Management, like a captain weathering storms at sea, must adeptly manage crises in external relations.
  By demonstrating resilience and strategic thinking, they ensure that the ship of the organization stays steady in the face of external challenges.

Navigating Trade Routes: Strategic Business Alliances and Partnerships:
- Strategic business alliances and partnerships are comparable to navigating trade routes. Leaders prioritize "Navigating Trade Routes: Strategic Business Alliances and Partnerships," recognizing the importance of strategically aligning with external entities for mutual benefit.
- Management, like a captain navigating trade routes, must strategically form business alliances and partnerships. By aligning with external entities, they enhance the organization's market position and open avenues for collaborative success.

Hoisting the Flag of Reputation: Managing the Organization's Image:
- Managing the organization's image is akin to hoisting the flag of reputation. Leaders prioritize "Hoisting the Flag of Reputation: Managing the Organization's Image," understanding that external perceptions profoundly impact success.
- Management becomes stewards of the organization's image, much like a captain hoisting the flag. By ensuring positive external perceptions through ethical practices

and effective communication, they navigate the organization towards a favorable standing in the external landscape.

Forming strategic partnerships.
Embarking on the journey of effective management with the Captain Mariner Mindset involves understanding the art of forming strategic partnerships. This guide explores the parallels between forming strategic partnerships and navigating the business seas, shedding light on how the captain's wisdom can guide leaders in creating positive waves through collaboration.

Charting the Course: Identifying Suitable Partners:
- Identifying suitable partners is akin to charting the course before setting sail. Leaders prioritize "Charting the Course: Identifying Suitable Partners," understanding that strategic alliances require careful consideration and planning.
- Management, like a captain charting the course, must identify partners aligning with the organization's goals. By carefully selecting collaborators, they set the foundation for a successful journey, ensuring synergy in the seas of strategic partnerships.

Navigating Turbulent Waters: Mitigating Risks in Partnerships:
- Mitigating risks in partnerships is comparable to navigating turbulent waters. Leaders prioritize "Navigating Turbulent Waters: Mitigating Risks in Partnerships," recognizing that challenges may arise, and a proactive approach is necessary for smooth sailing.
- Management, like a captain navigating turbulent waters, must mitigate risks in strategic partnerships. By anticipating challenges and having contingency plans, they ensure that the journey remains resilient, even in the face of unexpected waves.

Setting Sail Together: Aligning Goals and Objectives:
- Aligning goals and objectives is akin to setting sail together towards a common destination. Leaders prioritize "Setting Sail Together: Aligning Goals and Objectives," understanding that a shared vision is crucial for a successful partnership.
- Management, like a captain setting sail with a crew, must align goals and objectives with strategic partners. By fostering a shared vision, they create a collaborative environment that propels both parties towards mutual success.

Navigating Crosscurrents: Communication in Partnerships:
- Communication in partnerships is comparable to navigating crosscurrents. Leaders prioritize "Navigating Crosscurrents: Communication in Partnerships," recognizing that effective communication is essential for understanding and overcoming challenges.
- Management, like a captain navigating crosscurrents, must prioritize clear and open communication with strategic partners. By fostering transparent and timely communication, they ensure a smooth journey through the complex currents of collaboration.

Harvesting the Bounty: Mutual Benefits in Partnerships:
- Harvesting the bounty is akin to reaping mutual benefits from partnerships. Leaders prioritize "Harvesting the Bounty: Mutual Benefits in Partnerships," understanding that successful collaborations yield rewards for all involved.
- Management, like a captain harvesting the bounty of a successful voyage, must ensure that partnerships result in mutual benefits. By nurturing a symbiotic relationship, they create a positive and fruitful outcome for both parties involved.

Building a professional network.
In the vast expanse of effective management, the Captain Mariner Mindset extends beyond the organizational deck to emphasize the importance of building a professional network. This guide explores the parallels between networking and smooth sailing, illustrating how a captain's strategic

approach can be translated into effective management strategies for creating positive waves in professional relationships.

Casting the Net: Initiating and Cultivating Connections:
- Initiating and cultivating connections are akin to casting the net in the vast sea. Leaders prioritize "Casting the Net: Initiating and Cultivating Connections," understanding the need to actively seek and nurture professional relationships.
- Management, like a captain casting a net for a fruitful catch, must actively initiate and cultivate connections. By doing so, they expand their professional horizons, fostering collaborations that contribute to personal and organizational success.

Navigating the Currents: Adapting to Changing Networking Dynamics:
- Adapting to changing networking dynamics is comparable to navigating the currents. Leaders prioritize "Navigating the Currents: Adapting to Changing Networking Dynamics," recognizing the need for flexibility in networking approaches.
- Management, like a captain adjusting to changing currents at sea, must adapt to evolving networking dynamics. By staying attuned to industry shifts and adjusting their networking strategies accordingly, they ensure a steady course in the dynamic professional waters.

Harboring Alliances: Building Strategic Partnerships:
- Building strategic partnerships is akin to harboring alliances in a safe port. Leaders prioritize "Harboring Alliances: Building Strategic Partnerships," understanding the value of forming relationships that provide mutual support and benefit.
- Management, like a captain harboring alliances in a safe port, must strategically build partnerships. By fostering relationships with key individuals and organizations, they create a network that supports the organization's goals and objectives.

Charting New Courses: Exploring Diverse Networking Avenues:
- Exploring diverse networking avenues is comparable to charting new courses. Leaders prioritize "Charting New Courses: Exploring Diverse Networking Avenues," recognizing the importance of seeking connections beyond familiar territories.
- Management, like a captain exploring new courses for the ship's success, must venture into diverse networking avenues. By expanding their network beyond traditional circles, they gain access to fresh perspectives and opportunities.

Hoisting the Flag of Reputation: Managing Professional Image:
- Managing a professional image is akin to hoisting the flag of reputation in the professional world. Leaders prioritize "Hoisting the Flag of Reputation: Managing Professional Image," understanding that personal branding profoundly impacts success in networking.
- Management becomes stewards of their professional image, much like a captain hoisting the flag. By ensuring a positive personal brand through ethical practices, effective communication, and consistent networking efforts, they navigate their career towards a favorable standing in the professional landscape.

Chapter **33**

Ports of Call: Exploring Expansion
Evaluating new markets and opportunities.

In the seas of effective management, the Captain Mariner Mindset extends its influence to the art of exploring new markets and opportunities. Much like a seasoned captain navigating uncharted waters, leaders must master the skill of evaluating new markets and seizing opportunities. This guide illuminates the parallels between the captain's approach and effective management strategies for steering the organizational ship into unexplored territories.

Charting the Course: Identifying New Markets and Opportunities:
- Identifying new markets and opportunities is akin to charting the course through uncharted waters. Leaders prioritize "Charting the Course: Identifying New Markets and Opportunities," understanding the need for meticulous planning and navigation in unexplored territories.
- Management, like a captain charting a course, must systematically identify new markets and opportunities.
  By conducting thorough market research and staying attuned to industry trends, they lay the groundwork for successful navigation into unexplored business territories.

Testing the Waters: Market Research and Feasibility Analysis:
- Market research and feasibility analysis are comparable to testing the waters. Leaders prioritize "Testing the Waters: Market Research and Feasibility Analysis," recognizing that assessing the conditions is essential before committing resources.
- Management, like a captain testing the waters, must conduct thorough market research and feasibility analyses. By understanding the potential risks and rewards, they make informed decisions that ensure a smooth and successful entry into new markets.

Adjusting the Sails: Adaptability in Market Dynamics:
- Adaptability in market dynamics is akin to adjusting the sails to changing winds. Leaders prioritize "Adjusting the Sails: Adaptability in Market Dynamics," understanding the importance of flexibility in response to evolving market conditions.
- Management, like a captain adjusting the sails, must be adaptable to changing market dynamics.
  By staying agile and responsive, they ensure the organization is well-positioned to harness opportunities and navigate challenges in the ever-changing business landscape.

Navigating Trade Winds: Forming Strategic Alliances and Partnerships:
- Forming strategic alliances and partnerships is comparable to navigating favorable trade winds. Leaders prioritize "Navigating Trade Winds: Forming Strategic Alliances and Partnerships," recognizing the importance of collaborative efforts in maximizing opportunities.
- Management, like a captain navigating trade winds, must strategically form alliances and partnerships. By leveraging synergies with other entities, they harness the power of favorable business conditions to propel the organization forward in new markets.

Plotting a Steady Course: Strategic Planning for Market Entry:
- Strategic planning for market entry is akin to plotting a steady course through unfamiliar waters. Leaders prioritize "Plotting a Steady Course: Strategic Planning for Market Entry," understanding the need for a well-defined strategy before embarking on new ventures.
- Management, like a captain plotting a steady course, must engage in strategic planning for market entry. By setting clear goals, defining roles, and establishing a roadmap, they ensure a smooth and purposeful journey into new markets.

Strategic entry into new business areas.

The Captain Mariner Mindset extends its reach to strategic entry into new business areas. Much like a captain venturing into uncharted waters, leaders must adopt a strategic approach when exploring new opportunities. This guide explores the analogy between navigating uncharted waters and strategically entering new business areas, illustrating how a captain's mindset can be applied to create positive waves in business expansion.

Charting the Course: Comprehensive Market Analysis:

- Charting the course through uncharted waters is akin to conducting a comprehensive market analysis. Leaders prioritize "Charting the Course: Comprehensive Market Analysis," recognizing the need for a thorough understanding of the new business landscape.
- Management, like a captain charting a course, must conduct a comprehensive market analysis before entering new business areas. By understanding market dynamics, potential challenges, and opportunities, they ensure a well-informed and strategic entry.

Setting Sail with Purpose: Defining Clear Objectives and Goals:

- Setting sail with purpose in uncharted waters is comparable to defining clear objectives and goals. Leaders prioritize "Setting Sail with Purpose: Defining Clear Objectives and Goals," understanding that a clear direction is essential for successful navigation.
- Management, like a captain setting sail with purpose, must define clear objectives and goals before entering new business areas. By establishing a strategic direction, they guide the organization toward success and avoid drifting aimlessly in unfamiliar business territories.

Navigating Through Challenges: Mitigating Risks and Uncertainties:

- Navigating through challenges in uncharted waters is akin to mitigating risks and uncertainties. Leaders prioritize "Navigating Through Challenges: Mitigating Risks and Uncertainties," understanding the importance of risk management in unexplored business domains.
- Management, like a captain navigating challenges, must mitigate risks and uncertainties when entering new business areas.
  By implementing effective risk management strategies, they safeguard the organization against potential pitfalls and ensure a smoother journey.

Adopting Agile Navigation: Flexibility in Business Strategies:

- Adopting agile navigation in uncharted waters is comparable to flexibility in business strategies. Leaders prioritize "Adopting Agile Navigation: Flexibility in Business Strategies," recognizing the need to adapt to changing conditions.
- Management, like a captain adopting agile navigation, must be flexible in business strategies when entering new areas. By adapting to changing market conditions and customer demands, they steer the organization towards success in dynamic business environments.

Adapting management practices for different contexts.

In the realm of effective management guided by the Captain Mariner Mindset, the ability to adapt to different contexts is essential, much like a captain adjusting to diverse sea conditions. This guide explores the analogy between navigating diverse waters and adapting management practices for different contexts, highlighting the importance of flexibility and strategic decision-making in the pursuit of positive waves.

Sailing Through Different Climates: Recognizing Contextual Variations:

- Sailing through different climates on the sea mirrors recognizing contextual variations in business. Leaders prioritize "Sailing Through Different Climates: Recognizing Contextual Variations," acknowledging the dynamic nature of business environments.

- Management, akin to a captain adjusting to various climates, must recognize contextual variations. By understanding the unique challenges and opportunities presented by different contexts, they can tailor their approaches for optimal outcomes.

Adapting Leadership Styles: Tailoring Strategies to Different Teams:
- Adapting leadership styles to different crew dynamics is analogous to tailoring strategies to different teams. Leaders prioritize "Adapting Leadership Styles: Tailoring Strategies to Different Teams," understanding that one size does not fit all in leadership.
- Management, like a captain adapting to diverse crew dynamics, must tailor strategies to different teams. By recognizing the strengths, weaknesses, and preferences of each team, they foster an environment that maximizes productivity and morale.

Navigating Regulatory Seas: Complying with Different Business Environments:
- Navigating regulatory seas reflects complying with different business environments. Leaders prioritize "Navigating Regulatory Seas: Complying with Different Business Environments," recognizing the importance of adapting to diverse regulatory landscapes.
- Management, much like a captain navigating regulatory seas, must comply with different business environments' regulations.
  By staying abreast of legal requirements and cultural nuances, they ensure the organization sails smoothly through diverse regulatory waters.

Adjusting Decision-Making Processes: Flexibility in Approach:
- Adjusting decision-making processes mirrors the flexibility required in approach. Leaders prioritize "Adjusting Decision-Making Processes: Flexibility in Approach," understanding that decisions must align with the specific context.
- Management, like a captain adjusting the ship's course based on changing conditions, must be flexible in decision-making. By adapting to the specific context, they ensure decisions are well-suited to the organization's goals and the challenges at hand.

Chapter **34**

The Leadership Compass
Self-awareness and continuous self-improvement.

In the Captain Mariner Mindset, the concept of self-awareness and continuous self-improvement serves as the captain's personal compass, ensuring that leadership remains true to its course. This guide delves into the parallels between a captain's commitment to personal growth and the importance of self-awareness for effective management, creating positive waves in the professional seas.

Charting Your Course: Setting Personal and Professional Goals:
- Setting personal and professional goals is akin to charting your course as a captain. Leaders prioritize "Charting Your Course: Setting Personal and Professional Goals," understanding the importance of having a clear direction for personal growth.
- As a manager, adopting the Captain Mariner Mindset means setting clear goals for personal and professional development. By doing so, you create a roadmap for your journey towards becoming a more effective leader.

Sailing into Uncharted Territories: Embracing New Learning Opportunities:
- Embracing new learning opportunities is comparable to sailing into uncharted territories. Leaders prioritize "Sailing into Uncharted Territories: Embracing New Learning Opportunities," recognizing that personal growth often comes from exploring the unknown.
- As a manager, adopting the Captain Mariner Mindset involves a willingness to embrace new learning opportunities. By venturing into uncharted territories, you expand your knowledge and skills, contributing to your professional development.

Calibrating the Compass: Seeking Feedback for Continuous Improvement:
- Seeking feedback for continuous improvement is akin to calibrating the compass. Leaders prioritize "Calibrating the Compass: Seeking Feedback for Continuous Improvement," understanding that feedback is essential for staying on the right course.
- Managers adopting the Captain Mariner Mindset actively seek feedback to continuously improve.
  By calibrating their leadership compass through feedback, they navigate towards becoming more effective and impactful in their roles.

Weathering Personal Storms: Resilience in the Face of Challenges:
- Resilience in the face of challenges is comparable to weathering personal storms. Leaders prioritize "Weathering Personal Storms: Resilience in the Face of Challenges," understanding that personal challenges are inevitable on the journey of self-improvement.
- Managers adopting the Captain Mariner Mindset cultivate resilience. By weathering personal storms with grace and determination, they demonstrate strength in the face of challenges, contributing to their overall personal growth.

Navigating Emotional Tides: Emotional Intelligence in Leadership:
- Emotional intelligence in leadership is akin to navigating emotional tides. Leaders prioritize "Navigating Emotional Tides: Emotional Intelligence in Leadership," recognizing the impact of emotions on personal and professional interactions.
  Managers adopting the Captain Mariner Mindset cultivate emotional intelligence. By navigating emotional tides with empathy and self-awareness, they enhance their leadership effectiveness and contribute to a positive work environment.

Identifying and nurturing leadership traits.
In the vast ocean of effective management, identifying and nurturing leadership traits is akin to a captain cultivating the crew's unique skills for optimal performance. This guide delves into the

parallels between a captain's discernment in recognizing exceptional qualities in the crew and a manager's role in identifying and nurturing leadership traits to create positive waves in the organizational waters.

The Crew's Unique Talents: Recognizing Individual Leadership Potential:

- Recognizing individual leadership potential is comparable to a captain acknowledging the unique talents of each crew member. Leaders prioritize "The Crew's Unique Talents: Recognizing Individual Leadership Potential," understanding that every team member brings something valuable to the table.
- Managers adopting the Captain Mariner Mindset focus on identifying the leadership potential within their team. By recognizing individual strengths and talents, they can nurture these qualities to foster a team of effective leaders.

Watering the Seeds of Leadership: Providing Opportunities for Growth:

- Providing opportunities for growth is akin to a captain watering the seeds of leadership. Leaders prioritize "Watering the Seeds of Leadership: Providing Opportunities for Growth," understanding that leadership qualities flourish through experience and challenges.
- Managers adopting the Captain Mariner Mindset actively seek and create opportunities for their team members to grow as leaders. By providing challenges and responsibilities, they nurture the seeds of leadership within their team.

Guiding the Crew: Mentorship and Coaching for Leadership Development:

- Mentorship and coaching for leadership development are comparable to a captain guiding the crew through the seas. Leaders prioritize "Guiding the Crew: Mentorship and Coaching for Leadership Development," recognizing the importance of experienced guidance in leadership growth.

  Managers adopting the Captain Mariner Mindset actively engage in mentorship and coaching. By providing guidance and sharing experiences, they empower their team members to develop their leadership qualities.

Fostering a Leadership Culture: Creating an Environment of Empowerment:

- Creating an environment of empowerment is akin to a captain fostering a leadership culture among the crew. Leaders prioritize "Fostering a Leadership Culture: Creating an Environment of Empowerment," understanding that a culture that values leadership qualities benefits the entire organization.
- Managers adopting the Captain Mariner Mindset actively work towards fostering a leadership culture within their teams. By empowering individuals and promoting a culture that values leadership, they create a positive and impactful work environment.

The Compass of Values: Aligning Leadership Traits with Organizational Values:

- Aligning leadership traits with organizational values is comparable to a captain navigating by a compass aligned with true north.

  Leaders prioritize "The Compass of Values: Aligning Leadership Traits with Organizational Values," understanding the importance of ensuring leadership qualities align with the organization's core values.
- Managers adopting the Captain Mariner Mindset ensure that identified leadership traits align with the organization's values. By emphasizing values-driven leadership, they contribute to the overall success and positive impact of the team.

Developing a personal leadership style.

Much like a captain steering a ship through diverse waters, a manager must develop a personal leadership style that not only guides the team effectively but also creates positive waves in the organizational seas. This guide explores the analogy between a captain's unique approach to sailing and a manager's journey in developing a personal leadership style for smooth sailing in the realm of effective management.

Captain's Navigation Techniques: Crafting Your Leadership Approach:
- Crafting your leadership approach is akin to a captain refining navigation techniques based on the ship's characteristics and the sea's conditions. Leaders prioritize "Captain's Navigation Techniques: Crafting Your Leadership Approach," recognizing the need for a tailored style.
- Managers adopting the Captain Mariner Mindset understand that leadership is not one-size-fits-all. Crafting a personal leadership style involves assessing the team's dynamics, the organization's culture, and personal strengths to develop an approach that resonates with the unique challenges they face.

The Art of Delegation: Balancing Authority and Empowerment:
- Balancing authority and empowerment in delegation mirrors a captain's skill in assigning tasks while empowering the crew. Leaders prioritize "The Art of Delegation: Balancing Authority and Empowerment," recognizing that effective leadership involves entrusting others with responsibilities.
- Managers adopting the Captain Mariner Mindset master the art of delegation. By balancing authority with empowerment, they ensure that tasks are assigned strategically, allowing team members to take ownership and contribute to the success of the overall mission.
- and Decision-Making," recognizing the value of involving the team in key discussions.
- **Application:** Managers adopting the Captain Mariner Mindset engage in collaborative decision-making. By involving the team in important discussions, they leverage collective insights, fostering a sense of ownership and unity among team members.

Chapter **35**

Crosswinds: Embracing Diverse Perspectives
The value of different viewpoints.

In the vast sea of effective management, leaders embracing the Captain Mariner Mindset recognize the importance of navigating with diverse perspectives. This guide delves into the analogy of a captain valuing different viewpoints, drawing parallels to a manager's journey in appreciating the richness that diverse perspectives bring to the organizational voyage.

Captain's Lookout Points: Gaining Insights from Every Angle:
- A captain's lookout points symbolize the high vantage points where diverse perspectives converge. Leaders prioritize "Captain's Lookout Points: Gaining Insights from Every Angle," understanding that varied viewpoints enrich decision-making and contribute to organizational success.
- Managers adopting the Captain Mariner Mindset actively seek diverse perspectives within their team.
  By encouraging open dialogue and valuing input from team members with different backgrounds, experiences, and expertise, they ensure a comprehensive understanding of challenges and opportunities.

Navigating Cultural Currents: Recognizing the Strength of Diversity:
- Navigating cultural currents is akin to a captain recognizing the unique strengths brought by diverse crew members. Leaders prioritize "Navigating Cultural Currents: Recognizing the Strength of Diversity," acknowledging that a diverse team contributes to a robust and resilient organizational culture.
- Managers adopting the Captain Mariner Mindset actively foster an inclusive environment. They recognize the strengths that diverse perspectives bring to problem-solving, innovation, and creativity, creating a workplace culture that values and celebrates individual differences.

Steering Through Storms: Leveraging Diverse Skill Sets:
- Steering through storms parallels a captain leveraging diverse skill sets to navigate challenging conditions.
  Leaders prioritize "Steering Through Storms: Leveraging Diverse Skill Sets," understanding that a team with varied skills can successfully navigate complex challenges.
- Managers adopting the Captain Mariner Mindset strategically build teams with a mix of skills and expertise. By recognizing and utilizing the unique strengths of each team member, they enhance the overall capability of the team, ensuring effective problem-solving and resilience in the face of challenges.

Crew Collaboration: Building a Unified Front:
- Crew collaboration mirrors a captain orchestrating cooperation among individuals with different roles. Leaders prioritize "Crew Collaboration: Building a Unified Front," recognizing that cohesive teamwork is the foundation of successful leadership.
- Managers adopting the Captain Mariner Mindset cultivate an environment where collaboration is valued. By promoting teamwork and breaking down silos, they create a unified front where diverse talents work synergistically to achieve common goals, fostering a positive and productive workplace.

Charting Unexplored Territories: Innovating with Diverse Ideas:
- Charting unexplored territories parallels a captain embracing innovative ideas for new routes. Leaders prioritize "Charting Unexplored Territories: Innovating with Diverse Ideas," understanding that diversity sparks creativity and drives innovation.

- Managers adopting the Captain Mariner Mindset encourage a culture of innovation fueled by diverse ideas. By fostering an environment where team members feel empowered to share their unique perspectives, they unlock the potential for groundbreaking solutions and contribute to the organization's long-term success.

Fostering a constructive dialogue

In the sea of effective management, fostering a constructive dialogue among team members is akin to the captain navigating through diverse waters. This guide explores the analogy between a captain's ability to appreciate different viewpoints for strategic navigation and a manager's role in promoting a constructive dialogue that creates positive waves in the organizational seas.

Navigation by Multiple Compasses: The Strength of Diverse Perspectives:

- Navigating by multiple compasses mirrors a captain's reliance on diverse perspectives for strategic navigation. Leaders prioritize "Navigation by Multiple Compasses: The Strength of Diverse Perspectives," recognizing the value that different viewpoints bring to the decision-making process.
- Managers adopting the Captain Mariner Mindset understand that a team with diverse perspectives is a valuable asset. By appreciating and integrating various viewpoints, they navigate complex challenges with a comprehensive understanding, ensuring a well-rounded and informed decision-making process.

Charting Uncharted Waters: Embracing Innovation through Dialogue:

- Charting uncharted waters symbolizes a captain's embrace of innovation to navigate unfamiliar territories. Leaders prioritize "Charting Uncharted Waters: Embracing Innovation through Dialogue," understanding that fostering a constructive dialogue encourages the flow of innovative ideas within the team.
- Managers adopting the Captain Mariner Mindset create a culture where team members feel empowered to share innovative ideas. By encouraging open dialogue, they tap into the collective creativity of the team, leading to the discovery of new and inventive solutions to challenges.

Navigating through Stormy Seas: Constructive Conflict Resolution:

- Navigating through stormy seas reflects a captain's skill in steering the ship through challenges. Leaders prioritize "Navigating through Stormy Seas: Constructive Conflict Resolution," recognizing that conflicts are inevitable but can be navigated constructively through open dialogue.
- Managers adopting the Captain Mariner Mindset view conflicts as opportunities for growth. By fostering a constructive dialogue during challenging times, they navigate through conflicts with transparency and empathy, transforming them into catalysts for positive change and team development.

Clearing the Fog: Transparent Communication for Unity:

- Clearing the fog symbolizes a captain's need for transparent communication to ensure a clear path. Leaders prioritize "Clearing the Fog: Transparent Communication for Unity," understanding that open and honest dialogue is essential for fostering unity and trust within the team.
- Managers adopting the Captain Mariner Mindset prioritize transparent communication. By clearing any fog of uncertainty through open dialogue, they create an environment where team members feel heard, valued, and connected, contributing to a positive and cohesive team atmosphere.

Leveraging diversity for better decision-making.

Just as a seasoned captain draws on the strengths of a diverse crew to navigate the open sea, effective management harnesses the power of diverse perspectives for smooth decision-making. This guide explores the analogy between a captain leveraging the diversity of their crew and a manager embracing diverse viewpoints to chart a course for positive waves in the organizational voyage.

Unity in Diversity: The Crew's Strength in Decision-Making:

- A captain values the unique skills of each crew member to enhance decision-making. Similarly, leaders prioritize "Unity in Diversity: The Crew's Strength in Decision-Making," recognizing that diverse perspectives contribute to well-rounded and informed decisions.
- Managers adopting the Captain Mariner Mindset understand that a diverse team brings varied experiences and insights. By fostering an inclusive environment where all voices are heard, they ensure that decisions consider a broad spectrum of perspectives, leading to more robust and effective outcomes.

Sailing into Uncharted Waters: Innovative Solutions from Diverse Minds:

- A captain relies on diverse thinking to navigate unknown territories. Leaders prioritize "Sailing into Uncharted Waters: Innovative Solutions from Diverse Minds," acknowledging that innovation flourishes when individuals with different backgrounds collaborate.
- Managers adopting the Captain Mariner Mindset encourage a culture of innovation by tapping into the creativity of a diverse team. By embracing the unique viewpoints of team members, they inspire inventive solutions, steering the organization toward success in unexplored realms.

Navigating Through Decision Storms: Harnessing Diverse Strategies:

- A captain adjusts strategies based on diverse weather conditions. Leaders prioritize "Navigating Through Decision Storms: Harnessing Diverse Strategies," recognizing that diverse perspectives provide a range of strategies for overcoming challenges.
- Managers adopting the Captain Mariner Mindset view diverse strategies as valuable assets during decision storms.
  By considering a multitude of approaches, they navigate through uncertainties with resilience, ensuring the organization is prepared to weather any storm and emerge stronger.

The Constellation of Ideas: Illuminating Decision-Making through Diversity:

- Just as constellations guide a ship at night, diverse ideas light the path to effective decisions. Leaders prioritize "The Constellation of Ideas: Illuminating Decision-Making through Diversity," understanding that a variety of viewpoints illuminates the decision-making process.
- Managers adopting the Captain Mariner Mindset recognize that diverse ideas serve as guiding stars in decision-making. By fostering an environment where diverse perspectives shine, they ensure that decisions are well-informed, strategic, and aligned with the organization's goals.

Chapter 36

The Currents of Technology
Keeping up with technological trends.

Just as a seasoned captain embraces the latest navigation technology to enhance the ship's capabilities, effective management navigates the digital landscape by staying abreast of technological trends. This guide explores the analogy between a captain adapting to advanced navigation tools and a manager embracing technological trends for smooth sailing in the organizational voyage.

Charting a Course in the Digital Sea: Embracing Technological Navigation:
- A captain relies on cutting-edge navigation tools for precise course plotting. Leaders prioritize "Charting a Course in the Digital Sea: Embracing Technological Navigation," understanding that staying abreast of technology is crucial for precise organizational direction.
- Managers adopting the Captain Mariner Mindset recognize the importance of technology in organizational success.
  By integrating the latest technological tools, they ensure that the organization charts an informed course in the digital sea, leading to efficiency and competitiveness.

Digital Compass: Aligning Technological Trends with Organizational Goals:
- A captain aligns the ship's compass with the destination. Leaders prioritize "Digital Compass: Aligning Technological Trends with Organizational Goals," ensuring that technological advancements align seamlessly with the organization's mission.
- Managers adopting the Captain Mariner Mindset understand that technology is a tool, not a destination. By aligning technological trends with organizational goals, they navigate the digital landscape with purpose, leveraging innovations that propel the organization toward success.

Navigating Technological Turbulence: Adapting to Digital Currents:
- A captain adapts to changing currents for a smoother journey. Leaders prioritize "Navigating Technological Turbulence:
  Adapting to Digital Currents," acknowledging that technology evolves, and adaptability is key to smooth organizational sailing.
- Managers adopting the Captain Mariner Mindset stay vigilant to technological changes.
  By fostering a culture of adaptability, they ensure that the organization navigates technological turbulence with ease, embracing advancements that enhance operational efficiency.

Digital Lighthouse: Guiding the Organization through Innovation:
- A captain uses a lighthouse for navigation in the dark. Leaders prioritize "Digital Lighthouse: Guiding the Organization through Innovation," recognizing that technological innovation serves as a guiding light in the organizational journey.
- Managers adopting the Captain Mariner Mindset understand that innovation is fueled by technology. By fostering an environment that encourages digital creativity, they ensure the organization remains a beacon of progress, navigating through the digital landscape with confidence.

Sailing with Cybersecurity Anchors: Protecting the Ship from Digital Storms:
- A captain secures the ship with anchors during storms. Leaders prioritize "Sailing with Cybersecurity Anchors:
  Protecting the Ship from Digital Storms," understanding that technology comes with risks, and cybersecurity is the anchor that ensures organizational safety.

- Managers adopting the Captain Mariner Mindset prioritize cybersecurity in the digital age. By implementing robust cybersecurity measures, they safeguard the organization from potential digital storms, ensuring a secure and smooth voyage.

Integrating new technologies into business processes.

In the ever-evolving seas of business, adopting new technologies is akin to a captain integrating advanced navigation tools for a safer and more efficient journey. This guide explores the analogy between a captain seamlessly incorporating new technologies and a manager integrating innovation into business processes for effective management.

Charting a Course with Technological Compass: Embracing Innovation in the Organizational Map:

- A captain uses a compass for accurate navigation. Leaders prioritize "Charting a Course with Technological Compass: Embracing Innovation in the Organizational Map," understanding that innovation serves as a compass for organizational progress.
- Managers adopting the Captain Mariner Mindset recognize innovation as a guiding force. By actively seeking and incorporating new technologies, they ensure the organization charts a course towards efficiency and competitiveness in the business landscape.

Digital Infrastructure: Building a Sturdy Ship with Technological Foundations:

- A captain ensures the ship's structure is solid for a smooth voyage. Leaders prioritize "Digital Infrastructure: Building a Sturdy Ship with Technological Foundations," understanding that adopting new technologies forms the foundation for a resilient and agile organization.
- Managers adopting the Captain Mariner Mindset focus on building robust digital infrastructures. By investing in technological foundations, they fortify the organization against industry storms, ensuring it sails smoothly and adapts swiftly to changing business environments.

Sailing with Smart Navigation: Leveraging Technology for Strategic Decision-Making:

- A captain relies on smart navigation tools for strategic decision-making. Leaders prioritize "Sailing with Smart Navigation: Leveraging Technology for Strategic Decision-Making," recognizing that technology enhances the ability to make informed and timely decisions.
- Managers adopting the Captain Mariner Mindset integrate smart technologies into decision-making processes. By leveraging data analytics, artificial intelligence, and other cutting-edge tools, they steer the organization with precision, ensuring strategic goals are met and surpassed.

Technological Wind in the Sails: Enhancing Productivity through Automation:

- A captain adjusts sails to catch favorable winds. Leaders prioritize "Technological Wind in the Sails: Enhancing Productivity through Automation," acknowledging that automation and technology-driven processes propel the organization forward.
- Managers adopting the Captain Mariner Mindset embrace automation technologies. By integrating processes that enhance efficiency and reduce manual workload, they catch the technological wind, driving productivity and allowing the organization to sail ahead with momentum.

Balancing technology use with a human touch.

In the vast ocean of modern management, finding the delicate equilibrium between technology utilization and maintaining a human touch is akin to a captain harmonizing the ship's mechanical efficiency with the warmth of human interaction. This guide explores the analogy between a captain's balance at sea and a manager's art of harmonizing technology and human elements for effective and positive management waves.

Compassionate Navigation: Balancing the Technological Course with Human Understanding:

- A captain balances navigating through technology with a deep understanding of the sea. Leaders prioritize "Compassionate Navigation: Balancing the Technological Course with Human Understanding," acknowledging that effective management requires empathy and human connection.
- Managers adopting the Captain Mariner Mindset integrate technology into workflows while maintaining a compassionate understanding of their team.
  By valuing individual experiences and emotions, they ensure that technology complements human interactions rather than overshadowing them.

Digital Wind in the Sails, Human Touch at the Helm: Sailing Towards Success with a Human-Centric Approach:

- A captain adjusts sails for wind, but human hands steer the ship. Leaders prioritize "Digital Wind in the Sails, Human Touch at the Helm: Sailing Towards Success with a Human-Centric Approach," recognizing that technology augments but does not replace the human leadership essential for success.
- Managers adopting the Captain Mariner Mindset guide their teams with a human-centric approach while leveraging technology as a tool. By placing importance on personal connections and leadership, they ensure the ship sails towards success with both digital wind and human hands at the helm.

Empowering Crew with Technological Tools, Embracing Human Empowerment:

- A captain empowers the crew with advanced tools, but the human element remains crucial.
  Leaders prioritize "Empowering Crew with Technological Tools, Embracing Human Empowerment," understanding that technology should enhance, not replace, the capabilities of the workforce.
- Managers adopting the Captain Mariner Mindset empower their teams with technological tools while valuing the unique skills and insights each team member brings. By embracing human empowerment, they ensure that technology amplifies the crew's capabilities rather than overshadowing their contributions.

Chapter 37

Through the Spyglass: Future Forecasting
Anticipating market trends.

Just as a captain keenly observes the horizon for signs of changing weather, effective managers with the Captain Mariner Mindset vigilantly anticipate market trends, ensuring their organizations sail smoothly through the dynamic business seas. This guide explores the analogy between a captain's weather anticipation and a manager's foresight in predicting market shifts for creating positive waves in effective management.

The Business Barometer: Reading Market Signals like a Captain Reads the Sky:

- A captain observes the sky for weather cues; managers use data as their business barometer. Leaders prioritize "The Business Barometer: Reading Market Signals like a Captain Reads the Sky," understanding that data-driven insights are crucial for anticipating market trends.
- Managers adopting the Captain Mariner Mindset leverage data analytics to read market signals.
  By identifying patterns and trends, they anticipate shifts, enabling the organization to adjust its course proactively and navigate towards success.

Navigating through Economic Currents: Steering the Business Ship in Turbulent Markets:

- A captain navigates through currents; managers navigate through economic fluctuations. Leaders prioritize "Navigating through Economic Currents: Steering the Business Ship in Turbulent Markets," acknowledging that economic changes impact the business course.
- Managers adopting the Captain Mariner Mindset assess economic indicators. By understanding the financial currents, they make informed decisions, adjusting the business strategy to navigate effectively and ensure the ship remains resilient in turbulent markets.

Market Winds of Change: Adjusting Sails for Shifting Customer Preferences:

- A captain adjusts sails for winds; managers adjust strategies for changing customer preferences. Leaders prioritize "Market Winds of Change:
  Adjusting Sails for Shifting Customer Preferences," recognizing that customer trends direct the business journey.
- Managers adopting the Captain Mariner Mindset stay attuned to customer feedback and market trends. By adjusting sails—business strategies—they align with evolving customer preferences, ensuring the organization sails smoothly in the direction of market demand.

The Competitive Horizon: Scanning for Rivals as a Captain Scans for Nearby Ships:

- A captain watches for nearby ships; managers scan the competitive horizon. Leaders prioritize "The Competitive Horizon: Scanning for Rivals as a Captain Scans for Nearby Ships," understanding the importance of competitor analysis.
- Managers adopting the Captain Mariner Mindset continuously monitor the competitive landscape. By studying rivals and industry trends, they gain insights to stay ahead, ensuring the organization competes effectively and sails ahead in the business waters.

Seizing Opportunities in Uncharted Waters: Embracing Change for Business Expansion:

- A captain explores uncharted waters; managers embrace change for business expansion. Leaders prioritize "Seizing Opportunities in Uncharted Waters: Embracing

Change for Business Expansion," acknowledging that new opportunities often lie in unexplored territories.

- Managers adopting the Captain Mariner Mindset encourage a culture of adaptability. By fostering openness to change, they position the organization to seize opportunities in uncharted markets, ensuring a proactive approach to business expansion.

Future-proofing your business.

Similar to a captain preparing the ship for a variety of weather conditions, effective managers with the Captain Mariner Mindset embrace the importance of future-proofing their business. This guide delves into the analogy between a captain's preparations for unpredictable conditions at sea and a manager's strategies for navigating the uncertain business environment, ensuring a resilient and smooth journey.

The Navigational Chart: Strategic Planning as the Map for Business Resilience:
- A captain relies on navigational charts; managers use strategic planning as a map. Leaders prioritize "The Navigational Chart: Strategic Planning as the Map for Business Resilience," understanding the significance of having a clear roadmap.
- Managers adopting the Captain Mariner Mindset engage in strategic planning. By charting a course through market trends and potential challenges, they equip the business with a navigational chart, ensuring a resilient and adaptable route in the face of uncertainties.

Weathering Economic Storms: Financial Preparedness for Business Stability:
- A captain ensures the ship weathers storms; managers ensure financial preparedness. Leaders prioritize "Weathering Economic Storms: Financial Preparedness for Business Stability," recognizing the impact of economic turbulence.
- Managers adopting the Captain Mariner Mindset focus on financial resilience. By establishing robust financial practices and contingency plans, they prepare the business to weather economic storms, ensuring stability and minimizing the impact of financial uncertainties.

Crew Training and Skill Development: Building an Adaptable Workforce:
- A captain ensures the crew is skilled and adaptable; managers build an adaptable workforce. Leaders prioritize "Crew Training and Skill Development: Building an Adaptable Workforce," acknowledging the importance of a skilled and versatile team.
- Managers adopting the Captain Mariner Mindset invest in employee training.
  By nurturing a culture of continuous learning and skill development, they equip the workforce to navigate through changing landscapes, ensuring the business has a crew ready to face any challenge.

Technological Navigation: Leveraging Innovation for Long-Term Success:
- A captain uses navigation technology; managers leverage innovation. Leaders prioritize "Technological Navigation: Leveraging Innovation for Long-Term Success," recognizing the role of technology in business resilience.
- Managers adopting the Captain Mariner Mindset embrace technological advancements. By integrating innovative solutions and staying abreast of industry trends, they equip the business with the latest tools for long-term success, ensuring it sails smoothly into the future.

Strategic foresight.

Just as a captain scans the horizon for potential challenges and opportunities, effective managers with the Captain Mariner Mindset understand the importance of strategic foresight. This guide explores the analogy between a captain's vigilance in navigating uncharted waters and a manager's strategic foresight, ensuring the organization sets sail on a path of continuous success.

Charting Unexplored Waters: The Essence of Strategic Foresight:

- A captain scans the horizon for obstacles; managers cultivate strategic foresight. Leaders prioritize "Charting Unexplored Waters: The Essence of Strategic Foresight," recognizing the significance of anticipating and navigating potential challenges.
- Managers adopting the Captain Mariner Mindset actively engage in strategic foresight. By analyzing industry trends, predicting market shifts, and identifying emerging opportunities, they steer the organization away from potential obstacles and toward unexplored waters of growth.

Course Adjustments in Turbulent Tides: Agility in Strategic Decision-Making:

- A captain adjusts the ship's course in turbulent tides; managers adapt their strategies. Leaders prioritize "Course Adjustments in Turbulent Tides: Agility in Strategic Decision-Making," understanding the need for flexibility in the face of uncertainties.
- Managers adopting the Captain Mariner Mindset prioritize agility. By fostering a culture of adaptability and swift decision-making, they ensure the organization can navigate through turbulent tides, making strategic adjustments to stay on course toward success.

Navigating Economic Currents: Economic Trend Analysis for Business Stability:

- A captain reads economic currents; managers analyze economic trends. Leaders prioritize "Navigating Economic Currents: Economic Trend Analysis for Business Stability," acknowledging the impact of economic forces on organizational success.
- Managers adopting the Captain Mariner Mindset invest in economic trend analysis. By understanding and interpreting economic currents, they guide the organization to make informed decisions, ensuring stability and resilience against economic uncertainties.

Sailing into Competitive Waters: Competitor Analysis for Market Dominance:

- A captain assesses competitors at sea; managers analyze competitors in the market. Leaders prioritize "Sailing into Competitive Waters: Competitor Analysis for Market Dominance," recognizing the importance of understanding the competitive landscape.
- Managers adopting the Captain Mariner Mindset emphasize competitor analysis. By studying competitors' strategies, strengths, and weaknesses, they position the organization strategically, allowing it to sail into competitive waters with a clear advantage.

Chapter **38**

Ocean Conservation: Corporate Responsibility
The role of businesses in environmental conservation.

In the vast sea of corporate landscapes, the Captain Mariner Mindset extends beyond the organizational deck, recognizing the integral role businesses play in environmental conservation. This guide explores the analogy between a captain's responsibility to protect the seas and a business leader's commitment to environmental stewardship, ensuring the organization sails towards a sustainable and eco-friendly future.

Oceanic Responsibility: The Analogy of Corporate Stewardship:
- Just as a captain ensures the ocean's well-being, businesses uphold a responsibility to the environment. Leaders prioritize "Oceanic Responsibility: The Analogy of Corporate Stewardship," acknowledging the impact of business activities on the planet.
- Businesses adopting the Captain Mariner Mindset embrace environmental stewardship. By integrating sustainable practices, reducing carbon footprints, and prioritizing eco-friendly initiatives, they become stewards of the corporate ocean, contributing to a healthier planet.

Navigating Eco-friendly Strategies: Sailing Towards Sustainable Practices:
- A captain chooses eco-friendly routes; businesses adopt sustainable practices. Leaders prioritize "Navigating Eco-friendly Strategies: Sailing Towards Sustainable Practices," understanding the importance of aligning business operations with environmental preservation.
- Businesses adopting the Captain Mariner Mindset integrate eco-friendly strategies. By implementing sustainable practices such as waste reduction, energy efficiency, and responsible sourcing, they navigate towards a greener and more sustainable corporate journey.

Sustaining the Ecosystem: Biodiversity in Corporate Culture:
- A captain values marine biodiversity; businesses prioritize diversity in culture. Leaders prioritize "Sustaining the Ecosystem: Biodiversity in Corporate Culture," recognizing the parallels between ecological diversity and a diverse and inclusive organizational culture.
- Businesses adopting the Captain Mariner Mindset promote diversity and inclusion.
- By fostering a workplace culture that values and celebrates differences, they contribute to the sustainability of the corporate ecosystem, ensuring a vibrant and resilient organizational environment.

Tackling Climate Change: Navigating the Corporate Climate:
- A captain adjusts to changing weather; businesses adapt to climate change. Leaders prioritize "Tackling Climate Change: Navigating the Corporate Climate," acknowledging the business impact on and vulnerability to climate-related challenges.
- Businesses adopting the Captain Mariner Mindset develop strategies to address climate change. By setting emission reduction goals, embracing renewable energy sources, and implementing climate-resilient practices, they steer the organization towards a more climate-conscious and resilient future.

Beyond the Horizon: Corporate Social Responsibility as the True North:
- A captain looks beyond the horizon; businesses focus on Corporate Social Responsibility (CSR). Leaders prioritize "Beyond the Horizon: Corporate Social Responsibility as the True North," understanding the long-term benefits of socially responsible business practices.

- Businesses adopting the Captain Mariner Mindset prioritize CSR initiatives. By engaging in community outreach, supporting social causes, and contributing to philanthropic efforts, they navigate towards a horizon where businesses not only prosper but also contribute positively to society and the environment.

Eco-friendly business practices.

In the vast ocean of commerce, the Captain Mariner Mindset extends its compass towards eco-friendly horizons. This guide navigates the analogy between a seasoned captain's commitment to preserving the environment and a business leader's dedication to fostering eco-friendly practices. Join us on a journey to discover how businesses can sail towards sustainability, creating positive waves of effective environmental management.

Environmental Navigation: Charting the Course for Sustainable Operations:
- Just as a captain charts a course through the seas, businesses navigate towards sustainability. Leaders prioritize "Environmental Navigation: Charting the Course for Sustainable Operations," acknowledging the impact of business activities on the environment.
- Businesses adopting the Captain Mariner Mindset set sail towards sustainability by incorporating eco-friendly practices. This includes minimizing waste, reducing energy consumption, and sourcing responsibly, ensuring the business course aligns with the preservation of our planet.

Wind in the Sails: Harnessing Renewable Energy Sources:
- A captain harnesses the wind for propulsion; businesses leverage renewable energy. Leaders prioritize "Wind in the Sails: Harnessing Renewable Energy Sources," recognizing the importance of adopting clean and sustainable energy practices.
- Businesses adopting the Captain Mariner Mindset invest in renewable energy sources. Whether through solar, wind, or other eco-friendly alternatives, leaders steer their organizations towards a greener future, reducing their environmental impact and contributing to a sustainable energy landscape.

Waste Tides: Navigating the Waters of Waste Reduction:
- A captain minimizes waste at sea; businesses navigate the waters of waste reduction. Leaders prioritize "Waste Tides: Navigating the Waters of Waste Reduction," understanding the significance of minimizing their ecological footprint.
- Businesses adopting the Captain Mariner Mindset implement waste reduction strategies. This involves recycling, reusing materials, and adopting circular economy principles, ensuring that the organization contributes to cleaner seas and landscapes by minimizing waste.

Green Anchors: Sourcing Responsibly and Ethically:
- A captain drops anchor responsibly; businesses anchor themselves with ethical sourcing. Leaders prioritize "Green Anchors: Sourcing Responsibly and Ethically," understanding the impact of supply chain decisions on the environment.
- Businesses adopting the Captain Mariner Mindset engage in responsible and ethical sourcing practices. By choosing suppliers with eco-friendly practices, leaders ensure that their organization's anchor doesn't weigh down the environmental integrity, contributing to sustainable and ethical business ecosystems.

Engaging employees in sustainability.

In the vast expanse of corporate seas, the Captain Mariner Mindset extends its influence to the heart of every ship—the crew. In this guide, we explore how leaders can engage employees in sustainability, transforming them into passionate stewards of the environment. Embark on a journey where every team member contributes to the positive waves of effective management through a shared commitment to sustainability.

Crew Briefing: Communicating the Sustainability Mission:

- Just as a captain briefs the crew on the ship's mission, leaders communicate the sustainability mission. "Crew Briefing: Communicating the Sustainability Mission" emphasizes the importance of aligning every team member with the organization's commitment to environmental stewardship.

- Leaders adopting the Captain Mariner Mindset effectively communicate the sustainability goals, explaining how each team member contributes.
Through clear communication, employees understand the significance of their roles in creating positive environmental impact, fostering a shared sense of purpose.

Green Skill Training: Equipping the Crew for Sustainability:

- A captain ensures the crew has the skills for smooth sailing; leaders provide green skill training. "Green Skill Training: Equipping the Crew for Sustainability" focuses on developing the necessary skills and knowledge for employees to actively participate in sustainable practices.

- Leaders adopting the Captain Mariner Mindset invest in sustainability training programs. From waste reduction to energy conservation, employees are equipped with the tools needed to incorporate environmentally friendly practices into their daily work, fostering a culture of sustainability.

Eco-Friendly Deck Activities: Integrating Sustainable Practices:

- Just as a captain ensures ship activities align with sustainability, leaders integrate eco-friendly practices. "Eco-Friendly Deck Activities: Integrating Sustainable Practices" emphasizes incorporating sustainability into everyday work, making it a seamless part of the organizational culture.

- Leaders adopting the Captain Mariner Mindset integrate sustainable practices into daily operations. This includes eco-friendly office policies, energy-efficient technologies, and waste reduction initiatives. Employees actively engage in sustainability without disruption to their daily tasks, contributing to positive environmental change.

Green Team Spirit: Fostering a Culture of Collaboration:

- A captain values teamwork; leaders foster a green team spirit. "Green Team Spirit: Fostering a Culture of Collaboration" emphasizes the importance of collaborative efforts among employees to achieve sustainability goals.

- Leaders adopting the Captain Mariner Mindset encourage collaboration through green initiatives. Whether through team challenges, eco-friendly competitions, or shared sustainability goals, employees work together towards a common purpose, strengthening the overall commitment to sustainability.

Chapter 39

Mutiny Prevention: Retention Strategies
Understanding why employees leave.

In the vast sea of talent, captains of organizations must understand the tides that lead employees to set sail towards new horizons. This guide, inspired by the Captain Mariner Mindset, sheds light on comprehending the reasons behind employee departures, allowing leaders to navigate these waters and ensure smooth sailing towards a motivated and committed crew.

Casting Off: The Analogous Departure:
- Just as a ship sets sail, employees depart for new journeys. "Casting Off: The Analogous Departure" delves into the parallels between a ship embarking on a voyage and an employee leaving an organization.
- Leaders adopting the Captain Mariner Mindset view employee departures as a natural part of the professional journey. They acknowledge that individuals, like ships, chart their courses. Understanding this analogy helps leaders approach departures with a mindset of exploration rather than resistance.

Seafaring Feedback: Capturing the Winds of Dissatisfaction:
- A captain adjusts sails based on winds; leaders respond to feedback. "Seafaring Feedback: Capturing the Winds of Dissatisfaction" explores the importance of understanding employee feedback as a compass guiding organizational improvement.
- Leaders adopting the Captain Mariner Mindset actively seek and value feedback. They consider departures as signals, adjusting their course by addressing concerns and fostering an environment where employee concerns are heard and addressed, preventing further departures fueled by dissatisfaction.

Stormy Waters: Recognizing Organizational Challenges:
- A captain navigates storms; leaders recognize organizational challenges. "Stormy Waters: Recognizing Organizational Challenges" highlights the significance of identifying internal issues that may contribute to employee departures.
- Leaders adopting the Captain Mariner Mindset proactively identify and address challenges within the organization.
  By recognizing and navigating through turbulent waters, they create a workplace that retains talent, minimizing departures driven by internal organizational issues.

Anchors Aweigh: Untethering Employees for Professional Growth:
- A ship weighs anchor for new destinations; employees seek professional growth. "Anchors Aweigh: Untethering Employees for Professional Growth" explores how leaders can support employees in their pursuit of advancement.
- Leaders adopting the Captain Mariner Mindset understand that employees, like ships, may need to weigh anchor to explore new opportunities. They actively support professional development, creating an environment that encourages employees to grow within the organization or embark on new journeys, maintaining a positive relationship even as they depart.

The Compass of Recognition: Acknowledging Contributions:
- A captain acknowledges the crew's efforts; leaders recognize employee contributions. "The Compass of Recognition: Acknowledging Contributions" emphasizes the importance of appreciating and recognizing the valuable contributions of departing employees.
- Leaders adopting the Captain Mariner Mindset express gratitude for the contributions of departing team members.
  Recognizing their efforts ensures a positive departure, leaving the door open for potential future collaborations and maintaining a positive organizational reputation.

Strategies for employee retention.

Captains of organizations must employ effective strategies to retain their valuable crew members. This guide, inspired by the Captain Mariner Mindset, explores essential strategies for employee retention, ensuring smooth sailing and a cohesive, committed team.

Charting Loyalty Courses: The Crew's Commitment Compass:

- Just as a captain inspires loyalty, leaders cultivate commitment. "Charting Loyalty Courses" delves into the parallels between a captain fostering crew loyalty and a leader cultivating commitment among team members.
- Leaders adopting the Captain Mariner Mindset understand that employee retention begins with a commitment to their well-being. They actively build a positive workplace culture, recognizing and valuing the unique contributions of each team member, fostering loyalty and dedication to the organization.

Fair Winds of Recognition: Acknowledging and Rewarding Contributions:

- A captain rewards exceptional efforts;
- leaders recognize and reward outstanding contributions.
  "Fair Winds of Recognition" explores the importance of acknowledging and appreciating the efforts of team members to enhance retention.
- Leaders adopting the Captain Mariner Mindset actively implement recognition programs and reward systems. They ensure that employees feel valued for their hard work and dedication, creating an environment where individuals are motivated to stay and contribute to the organization's success.

Shore Leave: Balancing Work and Life Ports:

- Crews enjoy shore leave; employees need work-life balance. "Shore Leave" draws parallels between providing downtime for crews and ensuring employees have a healthy work-life balance.
- Leaders adopting the Captain Mariner Mindset prioritize work-life balance. They understand that well-rested and satisfied team members are more likely to stay committed. Offering flexibility, encouraging vacations, and respecting personal time contribute to employee satisfaction and retention.

Crew Development Expeditions: Investing in Skill Voyages:

- A captain invests in crew skills; leaders invest in employee development. "Crew Development Expeditions" explores the analogy between developing crew skills and fostering continuous learning and growth among team members.
- Leaders adopting the Captain Mariner Mindset actively invest in the professional development of their team. They provide opportunities for learning, mentorship, and skill enhancement, ensuring that employees are continually growing within the organization, strengthening their commitment and desire to contribute.

Safe Harbors of Communication: Open Dialogue Ports:

- A captain maintains open communication; leaders foster transparent dialogue. "Safe Harbors of Communication" emphasizes the importance of clear and open communication in retaining employees.
- Leaders adopting the Captain Mariner Mindset prioritize transparent communication. They establish regular feedback channels, actively listen to employee concerns, and address issues promptly. This open dialogue creates a sense of trust and belonging, enhancing employee retention.

Creating loyalty and a sense of belonging.

Leaders with the Captain Mariner Mindset recognize the crucial need to create a crew united by loyalty and a profound sense of belonging. This guide navigates the analogical waters, drawing parallels between a captain fostering crew loyalty and a leader building a dedicated team that feels deeply connected to the organization.

Anchoring Loyalty: A Captain's Creed in Leadership:
- A captain commands loyalty from the crew; leaders inspire loyalty through trust and shared values. "Anchoring Loyalty" explores the role of trust and shared values in fostering commitment and allegiance.
- Leaders adopting the Captain Mariner Mindset prioritize building trust with their teams. They communicate openly, align organizational values with individual aspirations, and demonstrate unwavering support. By embodying the values they seek, leaders forge a foundation of loyalty and dedication among team members.

Sailing the Seas of Recognition: Acknowledging Contributions:
- Just as a captain rewards exceptional efforts, leaders recognize and appreciate the contributions of their team.
"Sailing the Seas of Recognition" emphasizes the importance of acknowledging and celebrating individual and collective achievements.
- Leaders adopting the Captain Mariner Mindset create a culture of recognition. They celebrate milestones, both big and small, publicly acknowledging the efforts of their crew. This recognition reinforces a sense of pride and accomplishment, fostering loyalty and a shared sense of purpose.

Crew Brotherhood: A Sense of Belonging:
- Crew members form a brotherhood; employees seek a sense of belonging. "Crew Brotherhood" explores the parallels between the close-knit bonds among crew members and the need for employees to feel a strong sense of belonging.
- Leaders adopting the Captain Mariner Mindset prioritize creating a sense of community within the organization. They encourage collaboration, celebrate diversity, and foster an inclusive environment where every team member feels valued. This sense of belonging strengthens the emotional ties between individuals and the organization.

Compassionate Leadership: Navigating Employee Well-Being:
- A captain cares for the well-being of the crew; leaders prioritize employee well-being. "Compassionate Leadership" explores the importance of leaders actively caring for the physical and emotional welfare of their team.
- Leaders adopting the Captain Mariner Mindset prioritize employee well-being. They provide support systems, offer flexibility, and genuinely care about the challenges and aspirations of their team members. This compassionate approach creates a culture where employees feel cared for, enhancing their loyalty to the organization.

Tenure: The Longevity of Seas and Careers:
- A captain values experienced crew members; leaders recognize the importance of retaining seasoned employees. "Treasuring Tenure" explores the significance of valuing and retaining experienced team members.
- Leaders adopting the Captain Mariner Mindset invest in the growth and development of long-term employees. They provide opportunities for career progression, recognize the expertise of seasoned team members.

Chapter **40**

Personal Life Preserver
Managing personal stress for effective leadership.

Akin to a captain steering a ship, effective management requires navigating through the stress-laden waters. This guide, inspired by the Captain Mariner Mindset, explores strategies for managing personal stress, ensuring smooth sailing for leaders and their teams.

The Helm of Self-Care: The Captain's Personal Compass:

- A captain maintains the helm's functionality; leaders prioritize personal well-being. "The Helm of Self-Care" explores the parallels between a captain ensuring the helm's efficacy and leaders prioritizing their physical and mental well-being.
- Leaders adopting the Captain Mariner Mindset recognize the importance of self-care. They actively engage in practices that promote physical and mental wellness, understanding that a healthy leader is better equipped to guide their team through challenges and uncertainties.

Charting Emotional Tides: Navigating Through Emotional Resilience:

- A captain reads emotional tides; leaders cultivate emotional resilience. "Charting Emotional Tides" delves into the captain's ability to read sea emotions and leaders' cultivation of emotional resilience for effective decision-making.
- Leaders adopting the Captain Mariner Mindset develop emotional resilience. They understand that managing stress involves navigating emotional highs and lows. By cultivating resilience, leaders can make sound decisions, maintain composure, and inspire confidence in their team even during challenging times.

Clearing the Fog: Clarity Amidst Leadership Challenges:

- A captain navigates through fog; leaders seek clarity in challenges. "Clearing the Fog" draws parallels between a captain's navigation through obscured waters and leaders' pursuit of clarity when faced with complex challenges.
- Leaders adopting the Captain Mariner Mindset actively seek clarity. They approach challenges methodically, breaking them down into manageable parts
By maintaining focus and clarity, leaders can reduce stress, making informed decisions and guiding their teams through turbulent waters.

Anchors of Support: Building a Resilient Crew:

- A captain relies on a supportive crew; leaders build a resilient team. "Anchors of Support" explores the captain's reliance on a supportive crew and leaders' efforts to build resilient, supportive teams.
- Leaders adopting the Captain Mariner Mindset recognize the importance of a supportive team. They foster an environment where team members collaborate, communicate openly, and provide mutual support. A resilient team becomes an anchor during challenging times, alleviating stress for the leader.

Navigation Breaks: Incorporating Moments of Reprieve:

- A captain schedules navigation breaks; leaders incorporate moments of reprieve. "Navigation Breaks" emphasizes the importance of taking breaks for recharging, similar to a captain scheduling moments of rest during a journey.
- Leaders adopting the Captain Mariner Mindset understand the value of breaks.
They encourage a healthy work-life balance and recognize that moments of reprieve contribute to reduced stress and increased productivity. Taking breaks allows leaders to return to their roles with renewed focus and energy.

Identifying and mitigating burnout.

Just as a captain must ensure the well-being of their crew, effective leaders adopting the Captain Mariner Mindset recognize the importance of identifying and mitigating burnout. This guide explores strategies for safeguarding the mental and emotional health of the team, creating a resilient crew for the journey ahead.

Recognizing the Storm on the Horizon: Identifying Early Signs of Burnout:

- A captain spots distant storms; leaders recognize early signs of burnout. "Recognizing the Storm on the Horizon" draws parallels between a captain's ability to identify weather patterns and leaders' skills in recognizing the signs of burnout within their team.
- Leaders adopting the Captain Mariner Mindset actively observe their team's dynamics. They pay attention to changes in behavior, decreased productivity, and signs of fatigue. By recognizing early signs of burnout, leaders can proactively address issues and prevent further escalation.

Adjusting the Sails: Flexible Work Arrangements for Crew Well-being:

- A captain adjusts sails to weather conditions; leaders offer flexible work arrangements. "Adjusting the Sails" explores the captain's adaptability to weather conditions and leaders' flexibility in providing work arrangements that support the well-being of their team.
- Leaders adopting the Captain Mariner Mindset prioritize flexibility. They understand that each team member may face different challenges and offer customized solutions, such as flexible schedules or remote work options. This adaptability helps alleviate stress and contributes to a healthier work-life balance.

Shore Leave: Encouraging Well-deserved Breaks:

- A captain grants shore leave; leaders encourage well-deserved breaks. "Shore Leave" draws parallels between a captain allowing time off for the crew and leaders actively encouraging and facilitating breaks for their team.
- Leaders adopting the Captain Mariner Mindset recognize the importance of downtime. They encourage team members to take regular breaks, ensuring that everyone has the opportunity to recharge. This approach helps prevent burnout and promotes sustained high performance.

Crew Check-ins: Open Communication Channels for Emotional Well-being:

- A captain holds regular crew meetings; leaders foster open communication. "Crew Check-ins" explores the captain's practice of regular crew meetings and leaders' efforts to maintain open communication channels for the emotional well-being of their team.
- Leaders adopting the Captain Mariner Mindset prioritize open communication. They conduct regular check-ins with team members, creating a space for discussions about workload, challenges, and individual well-being. This practice builds trust and allows leaders to address concerns before they escalate.

Pursuing personal interests and hobbies.

In the Captain Mariner Mindset, effective leaders recognize the importance of balance between professional and personal life. Much like a captain pursuing personal interests during calm seas, leaders who engage in hobbies and personal pursuits can enhance their effectiveness in steering the ship of management. This guide explores the analogies and applications of incorporating personal interests into the leadership journey.

Casting a Personal Anchor: The Significance of Hobbies:

- Just as a captain may drop anchor to enjoy personal pursuits during calm waters, leaders can find stability through hobbies. "Casting a Personal Anchor" delves into the captain's temporary grounding and how leaders can similarly benefit from anchoring themselves in personal interests.

- Leaders adopting the Captain Mariner Mindset prioritize hobbies as a means of relaxation and rejuvenation. Engaging in personal interests provides a mental break, fostering creativity and resilience.
This approach allows leaders to return to their professional duties with renewed energy and perspective.

Sailing the Seas of Innovation: Fostering Creativity through Personal Pursuits:

- As a captain might find inspiration at sea, leaders can foster creativity through personal pursuits. "Sailing the Seas of Innovation" draws parallels between a captain's moments of inspiration and leaders gaining creative insights from their personal interests.
- Leaders adopting the Captain Mariner Mindset encourage team members to explore personal interests. By embracing diverse hobbies, individuals bring unique perspectives and creative solutions to the professional realm. This approach fosters innovation and contributes to a dynamic and adaptable team.

Navigating Self-Discovery: Unveiling Leadership Traits Through Personal Pursuits:

- A captain discovers strengths during personal pursuits; leaders unveil traits through hobbies. "Navigating Self-Discovery" explores how a captain's personal activities reveal hidden strengths, mirroring leaders' journeys of self-discovery through engaging in hobbies.
- Leaders adopting the Captain Mariner Mindset actively pursue personal interests to uncover hidden talents and strengths. By acknowledging and embracing these traits, leaders can apply them in their professional roles, contributing to their effectiveness and personal growth.

Weathering Storms: Personal Resilience Developed Through Hobbies:

- A captain builds resilience during personal pursuits; leaders develop personal resilience through hobbies. "Weathering Storms" highlights the captain's resilience and how leaders can similarly cultivate personal resilience through engaging in hobbies.
- Leaders adopting the Captain Mariner Mindset understand the importance of personal resilience. Hobbies provide a means of coping with stress and building emotional strength. This resilience, developed through personal pursuits, positively influences a leader's ability to navigate challenges in the professional sphere.

Chapter 41

Negotiating the Narrows
Negotiation skills for leaders.

In the Captain Mariner Mindset, effective leaders are akin to skilled negotiators steering their ship through the currents of collaboration and compromise. This guide explores the analogies and applications of negotiation skills, showcasing how leaders can adopt the captain's diplomacy for successful navigation in professional waters.

Navigating Collaboration: The Captain as Chief Diplomat:

- Just as a captain collaborates with various crew members, leaders are chief diplomats navigating collaboration. "Navigating Collaboration" delves into the captain's diplomatic role and how leaders can apply these skills in fostering teamwork and synergy.
- Leaders adopting the Captain Mariner Mindset prioritize collaboration by engaging in open communication, active listening, and promoting a culture of inclusivity. This approach ensures that each team member contributes to the collective success, mirroring the captain's diplomatic role on the ship.

Setting Sail for Win-Win Agreements: Negotiation as Charting a Course:

- A captain negotiates with nature to set sail; leaders negotiate for win-win agreements. "Setting Sail for Win-Win Agreements" explores the captain's negotiations with the elements and how leaders can similarly negotiate for mutually beneficial outcomes.
- Leaders adopting the Captain Mariner Mindset master the art of negotiation by focusing on creating win-win agreements. This involves identifying common goals, understanding stakeholders' perspectives, and finding solutions that satisfy all parties involved, leading to smoother sailing in the professional landscape.

Adapting to Turbulent Seas: Negotiating in Times of Change:

- A captain adapts to changing seas; leaders negotiate in times of change. "Adapting to Turbulent Seas" draws parallels between a captain's adaptability and a leader's negotiation skills during organizational changes.
- Leaders adopting the Captain Mariner Mindset understand the importance of negotiation during times of change.
  Whether navigating through market shifts or organizational restructuring, effective negotiation skills enable leaders to guide their teams through turbulent waters, fostering resilience and adaptability.

The Compass of Empathy: Understanding Stakeholder Needs:

- A captain empathizes with the crew; leaders understand stakeholder needs. "The Compass of Empathy" explores the captain's empathy for the crew and how leaders can develop a similar understanding of stakeholder needs through effective negotiation.
- Leaders adopting the Captain Mariner Mindset prioritize empathy in negotiations. Understanding the needs and concerns of stakeholders, whether internal teams or external partners, allows leaders to make informed decisions that benefit everyone involved. This approach builds trust and fosters positive relationships.

Charting a Clear Course: Effective Communication in Negotiations:

- A captain communicates clearly with the crew; leaders prioritize effective communication in negotiations. "Charting a Clear Course" emphasizes the importance of transparent communication and how leaders can employ this skill for successful negotiations.

- Leaders adopting the Captain Mariner Mindset prioritize effective communication to ensure a clear course in negotiations. Clear and transparent communication builds trust and minimizes misunderstandings, creating an environment where negotiations can thrive and reach successful resolutions.

Techniques for achieving win-win outcomes

In the realm of the Captain Mariner Mindset, effective leaders are adept negotiators, employing techniques that ensure a harmonious voyage for the entire crew. This guide illuminates the parallels between negotiation and sailing, offering insights into techniques for achieving win-win outcomes, essential for maintaining smooth sailing in the waters of effective management.

Sailing the Waters of Collaboration: Collaborative Negotiation Techniques:
- The captain collaborates with the crew; leaders engage in collaborative negotiation. "Sailing the Waters of Collaboration" explores negotiation techniques that mirror the captain's collaboration with the crew, fostering an atmosphere of teamwork.
- Leaders adopting the Captain Mariner Mindset use collaborative negotiation techniques such as brainstorming, joint problem-solving, and seeking input from all stakeholders. These techniques ensure that negotiations result in mutually beneficial agreements, mirroring the collaborative spirit aboard a well-run ship.

Navigating the Tides of Empathy: Empathetic Negotiation Approaches:
- The captain empathizes with the crew; leaders utilize empathetic negotiation approaches. "Navigating the Tides of Empathy" draws parallels between the captain's empathy for the crew and leaders' use of empathetic negotiation approaches.
- Leaders adopting the Captain Mariner Mindset employ empathetic negotiation techniques like active listening, understanding stakeholders' perspectives, and demonstrating genuine concern for their needs. By recognizing and addressing the emotions and concerns of all parties involved, leaders can steer negotiations toward win-win outcomes.

Synchronizing Goals: Integrative Negotiation Strategies:
- A captain aligns goals with the crew; leaders implement integrative negotiation strategies. "Synchronizing Goals" explores the captain's role in aligning goals and how leaders can implement integrative negotiation strategies for mutual benefit.
- Leaders adopting the Captain Mariner Mindset use integrative negotiation strategies like expanding the pie, finding common ground, and emphasizing shared objectives. These techniques facilitate the creation of win-win outcomes where both parties feel their goals are achieved without compromising the other's.

Weathering Storms: Principled Negotiation in Turbulent Times:
- A captain adapts to changing seas; leaders employ principled negotiation during turbulence. "Weathering Storms" draws parallels between a captain's adaptability and leaders' use of principled negotiation in times of change.
- Leaders adopting the Captain Mariner Mindset utilize principled negotiation techniques such as separating people from the problem, focusing on interests rather than positions, and generating options for mutual gain. These techniques help leaders navigate through turbulent negotiations, ensuring that both sides emerge with positive outcomes.

Preparing for and conducting negotiations.

In the Captain Mariner Mindset, effective leaders are seasoned negotiators, capable of steering their teams through the unpredictable tides of business dealings. This guide draws parallels between a captain's preparation for and execution of a voyage and a leader's approach to negotiations, offering insights into preparing for and conducting negotiations with finesse.

Charting the Course: Preparing for Negotiations like Plotting a Voyage:
- Just as a captain meticulously plans a route, leaders prepare for negotiations. "Charting the Course" delves into the importance of strategic planning before entering negotiations.
- Leaders adopting the Captain Mariner Mindset understand the significance of meticulous preparation. They identify negotiation goals, research counterparties, and anticipate potential challenges. This step mirrors a captain's preparation, ensuring a clear route and minimizing surprises during the negotiation voyage.

Setting Sail: Initiating Negotiations with Confidence:
- A captain sets sail with confidence; leaders initiate negotiations boldly. "Setting Sail" explores the parallels between a captain's confident embarkation and a leader's initiation of negotiations.
- Leaders adopting the Captain Mariner Mindset approach negotiations with confidence. They initiate discussions with clarity, establishing rapport with counterparties, and clearly articulating their objectives. This approach sets a positive tone for the negotiation journey.

Navigating the Waters: Active Adaptation During Negotiations:
- A captain adjusts the course mid-voyage; leaders adapt during negotiations. "Navigating the Waters" highlights the need for flexibility and adaptability in the midst of negotiations.
- Leaders adopting the Captain Mariner Mindset stay agile during negotiations. They remain attentive to shifts in the conversation, adjusting their strategies based on emerging dynamics. This mirrors a captain adjusting the course to navigate changing sea conditions, ensuring the negotiation remains on course.

Weathering Storms: Managing Conflicts and Challenges:
- A captain faces storms at sea; leaders manage conflicts in negotiations. "Weathering Storms" explores how leaders navigate conflicts during negotiations, akin to a captain facing turbulent weather.
- Leaders adopting the Captain Mariner Mindset employ conflict resolution strategies. They address challenges head-on, encouraging open communication, and finding common ground. This approach ensures that negotiations, like a ship in a storm, can weather challenges and continue toward a successful resolution.

Docking Safely: Concluding Negotiations with Mutual Satisfaction:
- A captain safely docks the ship; leaders conclude negotiations successfully. "Docking Safely" underscores the importance of a safe and satisfactory conclusion to negotiations.
- Leaders adopting the Captain Mariner Mindset prioritize a mutually beneficial resolution. They ensure all parties leave the negotiation table with a sense of accomplishment.

Chapter 42

Cresting the Leadership Wave
Current leadership trends and challenges.

In the ever-changing seas of leadership, the Captain Mariner Mindset serves as a compass, guiding leaders through current trends and challenges. This guide draws parallels between a captain's mastery of navigating ocean currents and a leader's approach to understanding and overcoming contemporary leadership challenges.

Reading the Tides: Staying Informed on Leadership Trends:
- A captain reads the tides for a safe voyage; leaders stay informed on leadership trends for effective management. "Reading the Tides" explores the importance of keeping abreast of the latest trends in leadership.
- Leaders adopting the Captain Mariner Mindset prioritize continuous learning. They stay informed about emerging leadership trends, adapting their strategies to the ever-evolving business landscape. This approach ensures they can effectively navigate the currents of modern leadership challenges.

Charting Unfamiliar Waters: Navigating New Leadership Models:
- A captain charts unfamiliar waters; leaders navigate new leadership models. "Charting Unfamiliar Waters" delves into the necessity of adapting to novel leadership paradigms.
- Leaders adopting the Captain Mariner Mindset are open to exploring innovative leadership models. They chart new waters by embracing flexible organizational structures, diverse team dynamics, and cutting-edge management philosophies. This approach enables them to navigate the uncharted currents of modern leadership.

Stormy Weather: Addressing Leadership Challenges Head-On:
- A captain faces stormy weather at sea; leaders address leadership challenges head-on. "Stormy Weather" examines how leaders confront and overcome the challenges posed by the volatile currents of leadership.
- Leaders adopting the Captain Mariner Mindset are resilient in the face of challenges. They acknowledge and address leadership hurdles promptly, employing effective strategies to weather the storm.
  This approach ensures that leaders can navigate turbulent leadership waters with confidence and composure.

Crew Morale: Fostering Positive Work Environments:
- A captain ensures crew morale for a successful voyage; leaders foster positive work environments. "Crew Morale" explores the correlation between a captain's focus on crew well-being and a leader's role in creating positive workplaces.
- Leaders adopting the Captain Mariner Mindset prioritize the well-being and morale of their teams. They create positive work environments by promoting open communication, recognizing achievements, and fostering a sense of belonging. This approach ensures that the team sails smoothly through the sometimes choppy waters of modern workplaces.

Sustainability in Leadership: Navigating Ethical Waters:
- A captain navigates ethically; leaders ensure sustainability in leadership. "Sustainability in Leadership" explores the importance of ethical considerations in leadership.
- Leaders adopting the Captain Mariner Mindset prioritize ethical leadership
  They navigate the waters of corporate responsibility, ensuring sustainability and ethical practices guide their decision-making. This approach ensures leaders steer their organizations through ethically sound waters, fostering trust and credibility.

Preparing for the next wave of management innovations.

As the business seas evolve, effective leaders, adopting the Captain Mariner Mindset, prepare for the next wave of management innovations. Drawing inspiration from a captain's strategic approach to changing tides, this guide explores how leaders can anticipate and leverage upcoming management trends.

Scanning the Horizon: Anticipating Management Trends Like a Captain:

- A captain scans the horizon for upcoming challenges; leaders anticipate management trends. "Scanning the Horizon" emphasizes the importance of foresight in preparing for the next wave of innovations.
- Leaders adopting the Captain Mariner Mindset actively scan the business horizon for emerging management trends. They invest time and resources in market research, keeping an eye on industry shifts, technological advancements, and evolving customer expectations. This approach ensures they are well-prepared to navigate the seas of change.

R&D for Leadership: Innovating Like a Captain in Uncharted Waters:

- A captain innovates in uncharted waters; leaders engage in R&D for leadership. "R&D for Leadership" explores the necessity of investing in leadership innovation.
- Leaders adopting the Captain Mariner Mindset prioritize Research and Development (R&D) for leadership. They invest in training programs, leadership development initiatives, and mentorship structures to foster innovative management practices. This approach ensures they are well-equipped to steer through uncharted waters, adapting to evolving business landscapes.

Agility in Leadership Navigation: Responding Swiftly to Change:

- A captain navigates with agility in changing conditions; leaders respond swiftly to management changes. "Agility in Leadership Navigation" highlights the importance of adaptability in the face of dynamic management trends.
- Leaders adopting the Captain Mariner Mindset prioritize agility in leadership. They create flexible organizational structures, empower teams to embrace change, and foster a culture of continuous improvement. This approach ensures leaders can navigate the ever-changing currents of management trends with grace and efficiency.

Collaborative Navigation: Steering Towards Collective Change Change:

- A captain collaborates with the crew for effective navigation; leaders foster collaborative innovation. "Collaborative Navigation" explores the benefits of collective efforts in steering towards innovative solutions.
- Leaders adopting the Captain Mariner Mindset encourage collaborative innovation. They create cross-functional teams, facilitate open communication, and value diverse perspectives within their organizations. This approach ensures that the entire crew contributes to steering the ship towards innovative management practices.

Continuous learning as a leader.

In the Captain Mariner Mindset, effective leaders recognize the vast expanse of knowledge and understand that continuous learning is the compass guiding them to success. This guide draws parallels between a captain's commitment to mastering the seas and a leader's dedication to perpetual learning, emphasizing the pivotal role of continuous education in navigating the complex waters of effective management.

Charting Unexplored Territories: The Captain's Quest for Wisdom:

- Just as a captain charts unexplored territories, leaders embark on a continuous quest for wisdom. "Charting Unexplored Territories" underscores the significance of exploring new knowledge domains.
- Leaders with the Captain Mariner Mindset cultivate a thirst for knowledge. They actively seek out learning opportunities, attend conferences, enroll in courses, and

engage with thought leaders. This approach ensures leaders stay ahead by exploring uncharted territories in leadership and management.

Navigating Challenging Waters: Learning from Setbacks and Challenges:

- A captain learns from challenging waters; leaders gain insights from setbacks. "Navigating Challenging Waters" highlights the invaluable lessons found in overcoming obstacles.
- Leaders adopting the Captain Mariner Mindset view challenges as learning opportunities. They reflect on setbacks, analyze failures, and extract valuable insights. This approach ensures that leaders not only weather storms but emerge stronger and more resilient, equipped with the knowledge to tackle future challenges.

Harnessing the Winds of Change: Adapting to Evolving Leadership Trends:

- A captain adapts to changing winds; leaders evolve with leadership trends. "Harnessing the Winds of Change" stresses the importance of staying attuned to evolving leadership practices.
- Leaders with the Captain Mariner Mindset embrace change in leadership trends. They stay informed about the latest management methodologies, leadership theories, and industry best practices. This approach ensures leaders remain agile, steering their organizations with strategies aligned to the currents of contemporary leadership.

The Captain's Library: Building a Repository of Leadership Knowledge:

- A captain accumulates knowledge in a ship's library; leaders build a repository of leadership wisdom. "The Captain's Library" emphasizes the value of creating a personal reservoir of leadership insights.
- Leaders adopting the Captain Mariner Mindset curate their leadership libraries. They collect books, articles, and resources that contribute to their understanding of effective leadership. This approach ensures leaders have a wealth of knowledge at their fingertips, ready to inform their decisions and strategies.

Chapter **43**

Light: Ethics and Transparency
Importance of ethical leadership.

In the vast ocean of leadership, the Captain Mariner Mindset places ethical leadership at the helm, ensuring a course set for integrity and sustainable success. "Navigating Ethical Waters" draws parallels between a captain's commitment to ethical navigation and a leader's dedication to fostering an environment where ethical principles guide every decision and action.

The Moral Compass: Setting a Course of Integrity:
- Just as a captain relies on a moral compass, leaders must set a course guided by integrity. "The Moral Compass" underscores the significance of ethical principles as the guiding force.
- Leaders with the Captain Mariner Mindset prioritize ethical decision-making. They establish clear ethical guidelines for themselves and their teams, ensuring that every action aligns with a moral compass. This approach ensures a steady and principled course in the face of ethical challenges.

Weathering Ethical Storms: Resilience in the Face of Moral Challenges:
- A captain weathers storms with resilience; leaders face ethical challenges with steadfastness. "Weathering Ethical Storms" highlights the importance of resilience in maintaining ethical standards.
- Leaders adopting the Captain Mariner Mindset demonstrate resilience in upholding ethical values. They address ethical challenges promptly, learn from them, and use these experiences to fortify their commitment to ethical leadership. This approach ensures that ethical storms do not derail the ship but strengthen its ethical foundation.

Building Trustworthy Crews: The Importance of Ethical Team Dynamics:
- A captain trusts the crew; leaders build trustworthy teams. "Building Trustworthy Crews" emphasizes the pivotal role of ethical team dynamics in fostering trust.
- Leaders with the Captain Mariner Mindset prioritize the cultivation of an ethical work culture. They nurture an environment where trust is paramount, fostering collaboration, open communication, and mutual respect.
  This approach ensures that every crew member operates with the same commitment to ethical leadership.

Anchored in Values: Embedding Ethics in Organizational Culture:
- A captain's values anchor the ship; leaders embed ethics in organizational culture. "Anchored in Values" stresses the importance of infusing ethical principles into the fabric of an organization.
- Leaders adopting the Captain Mariner Mindset instill ethical values in the organizational culture. They lead by example, promote transparency, and establish systems that prioritize ethical decision-making. This approach ensures that the organization remains anchored in a culture of integrity.

Ethical Navigation through Uncertain Waters: Guiding Principles in Decision-Making:
- A captain navigates through uncertainty with guiding principles; leaders use ethics in decision-making. "Ethical Navigation through Uncertain Waters" highlights the use of ethical principles as a guide in challenging decisions.
- Leaders with the Captain Mariner Mindset rely on ethical principles as beacons in decision-making. They weigh the impact of decisions on all stakeholders, ensuring that ethical considerations are paramount, especially in uncertain and challenging situations. This approach ensures a steady course even in the face of uncertainty.

Fostering transparency and openness.

In the vast expanse of leadership, the Captain Mariner Mindset places transparency and openness as guiding stars. "Transparent Seas" draws parallels between a captain's transparent communication and a leader's commitment to fostering an open environment, ensuring smooth sailing and positive waves of effective management.

The Clear Horizon: Setting a Vision of Transparency:

- A captain's clear view of the horizon; leaders set a vision of transparency. "The Clear Horizon" underscores the importance of a transparent vision in leadership.
- Leaders adopting the Captain Mariner Mindset cultivate a transparent vision. They communicate organizational goals clearly, ensuring every crew member understands their role. This approach creates a shared vision, fostering a sense of purpose and direction among the team.

Open Communication Channels: Navigating Through Clear Waters:

- Navigating through clear waters; leaders open communication channels. "Open Communication Channels" highlights the significance of transparent communication in leadership.
- Leaders with the Captain Mariner Mindset prioritize open communication. They establish clear channels for feedback, questions, and concerns, creating an environment where information flows freely. This approach ensures that the team is well-informed, minimizing misunderstandings and fostering collaboration.

Charting the Course Together: Inclusive Decision-Making:

- Crew involvement in navigation; leaders include teams in decision-making. "Charting the Course Together" emphasizes the inclusivity of decision-making processes.
- Leaders adopting the Captain Mariner Mindset involve teams in decision-making. They seek input, encourage diverse perspectives, and value every team member's insights. This approach promotes a sense of ownership and shared responsibility, fostering a culture of openness.

Weathering Storms with Transparency: Honest Communication in Challenges:

- Honest communication in storms; leaders transparently address challenges. "Weathering Storms with Transparency" highlights the importance of open communication during challenging times.
- Leaders with the Captain Mariner Mindset communicate openly during challenges. They share information transparently, address concerns promptly, and acknowledge uncertainties. This approach builds trust and resilience within the team, ensuring that challenges are navigated with honesty and transparency.

Clearing the Fog: Transparent Decision-Making Processes:

- Clearing fog for navigation; leaders ensure transparent decision-making. "Clearing the Fog" emphasizes the need for clarity in decision-making processes.
- Leaders adopting the Captain Mariner Mindset ensure transparent decision-making processes. They communicate the rationale behind decisions, share relevant information, and provide clarity on the decision-making journey. This approach minimizes ambiguity and fosters trust among the team.

Handling ethical breaches.

"Navigating Ethical Waters" sets sail into the intricate realm of leadership, drawing parallels between a captain's commitment to ethical navigation and a leader's responsibility to uphold integrity. In the vast sea of management, ethical breaches can create turbulent waters. This guide embraces the Captain Mariner Mindset to steer through these challenges and ensure positive waves of effective management.

The Moral Compass: Setting Ethical Standards:

- A captain's reliance on a compass; leaders set ethical standards as their moral compass. "The Moral Compass" underscores the importance of establishing and communicating clear ethical guidelines.
- Leaders adopting the Captain Mariner Mindset set unwavering ethical standards. They communicate these standards to the team, emphasizing the non-negotiable importance of integrity in all actions. This approach serves as a guiding light, helping the team navigate the often-murky waters of ethical decision-making.

Ethical Navigation: Decision-Making in Uncharted Territory:

- A captain's strategic decisions in uncharted waters; leaders navigate ethical dilemmas with care. "Ethical Navigation" focuses on the complexities of decision-making in unfamiliar ethical terrain.
- Leaders with the Captain Mariner Mindset approach ethical dilemmas strategically. They gather relevant information, consult the moral compass, and involve key stakeholders in decision-making. This ensures that even in uncharted ethical waters, decisions are made with integrity and consideration.

Open Communication in Troubled Waters: Addressing Ethical Breaches Transparently:

- Open communication during turbulent seas; leaders address ethical breaches transparently. "Open Communication in Troubled Waters" emphasizes the importance of transparently dealing with ethical breaches.
- Leaders adopting the Captain Mariner Mindset prioritize open communication when ethical breaches occur. They address issues promptly, share information transparently with the team, and outline steps taken to rectify the situation.
  This approach fosters trust and demonstrates a commitment to ethical integrity.

Anchoring Accountability: Holding the Crew Responsible:

- Anchoring the ship for stability; leaders anchor accountability to maintain stability after ethical breaches. "Anchoring Accountability" highlights the necessity of holding individuals responsible for their actions.
- Leaders with the Captain Mariner Mindset ensure accountability after ethical breaches. They establish clear consequences for unethical behavior, creating a culture where every member understands the weight of their actions. This approach strengthens the foundation of integrity within the team.

Repairing the Ship: Restoring Trust After Ethical Breaches:

- Repairing the ship after a storm; leaders restore trust after ethical breaches. "Repairing the Ship" focuses on rebuilding trust and confidence within the team.
- Leaders adopting the Captain Mariner Mindset take proactive steps to restore trust. They implement corrective actions, engage in transparent communication, and demonstrate a renewed commitment to ethical conduct.

Chapter **44**

Conclusion: The Captain's Journey
Recap of key management practices.

"Charting the Course" offers a comprehensive recap of the key management practices from the Captain Mariner Mindset. Drawing inspiration from the world of maritime leadership, this guide consolidates the essential principles for effective management. Let's navigate through the key practices that ensure a smooth sailing journey in the realm of leadership.

Setting Sail with Purpose: Defining Clear Goals and Objectives:
- Hoisting the sails for a purposeful journey; leaders set sail with clear goals and objectives. "Setting Sail with Purpose" underscores the importance of defining a direction for the team.
- Leaders embracing the Captain Mariner Mindset start by establishing clear goals. They communicate these objectives to the crew, ensuring everyone understands the destination and the purpose of the journey.

Navigating Ethical Waters: Upholding Integrity and Transparency:
- Ethical navigation as the ship's moral compass; leaders navigate ethical waters with integrity. "Navigating Ethical Waters" focuses on upholding ethical standards and transparency.
- Leaders prioritize ethical decision-making, setting clear ethical standards as their moral compass. They communicate transparently with the team, fostering a culture of trust and integrity.

Steering Through Team Dynamics: Building and Sustaining a Cohesive Crew:
- Steering through the dynamics of the sea; leaders navigate team dynamics to build cohesion. "Steering Through Team Dynamics" emphasizes the importance of effective teamwork.
- Leaders adopting the Captain Mariner Mindset recognize the significance of teamwork. They foster collaboration, address conflicts promptly, and ensure that the crew works seamlessly together toward common goals.

Weathering Storms: Crisis Management and Composure Under Pressure:
- Weathering storms at sea; leaders manage crises with composure. "Weathering Storms" focuses on crisis management and maintaining composure under pressure.
- Leaders stay composed during challenging times, implementing effective crisis management strategies. They provide guidance, reassurance, and adapt to changing circumstances to ensure a steady course.

Sailing on the Winds of Communication: Active Listening and Clear Communication:
- Sailing on the winds of effective communication; leaders prioritize active listening. "Sailing on the Winds of Communication" focuses on the importance of clear communication.
- Leaders actively listen to their crew, encouraging open communication. They convey information clearly, ensuring that messages are understood, and actively seek feedback to enhance communication.

Nurturing the Crew: Encouraging Growth and Development:
- Nurturing the crew for long-term success; leaders encourage individual and team growth. "Nurturing the Crew" highlights the importance of professional development.
- Leaders prioritize the growth of their team members, providing opportunities for learning and development. They recognize achievements, foster a culture of continuous improvement, and encourage self-improvement.

Final thoughts on leadership and creating positive waves.

In the concluding chapter, "Casting a Legacy," we explore the final thoughts on leadership within the Captain Mariner Mindset. This segment encapsulates the essence of effective management and leaves behind a legacy of positive waves in the organizational seas.

Navigating the Seas of Leadership:

- Navigating the seas of leadership; leaders are akin to experienced captains steering through ever-changing waters. "Navigating the Seas of Leadership" emphasizes the continuous nature of leadership and the need for adaptability.
- True leaders acknowledge that leadership is an ongoing journey. They adapt their strategies, learn from experiences, and consistently hone their skills, ensuring that they remain effective guides for their teams.

The Ripple Effect of Positivity:

- The ripple effect of positivity; leaders understand that their attitude influences the entire crew.
  "The Ripple Effect of Positivity" focuses on the impact of a leader's demeanor on team morale and productivity.
- Leaders within the Captain Mariner Mindset recognize the power of positivity. By radiating optimism, gratitude, and resilience, they create a ripple effect that permeates the entire team, fostering a harmonious and motivated work environment.

Sailing into the Future:

- Sailing into the future; leaders cast their vision beyond the horizon. "Sailing into the Future" underscores the importance of visionary leadership.
- Visionary leaders look beyond immediate challenges. They inspire the crew with a compelling vision, steering the organization toward long-term success and ensuring that every decision aligns with the ultimate destination.

Legacy of Leadership:

- Leaving a lasting legacy; leaders focus on building a legacy that outlasts their tenure. "Legacy of Leadership" delves into the significance of creating a lasting impact.
- Leaders in the Captain Mariner Mindset strive to leave a positive mark on their teams and organizations. They invest in the development of their people, foster a culture of trust and innovation, and ensure that their leadership journey contributes to a sustainable legacy.

Encouragement for the ongoing journey of effective management.

Final Analogical Guide on Leadership and Encouragement for the Ongoing Journey of Effective Management

Setting the Sail for the Ongoing Voyage:

- As a captain sets sail for a continuous journey, leaders embrace the ongoing nature of effective management. The seas of leadership are vast, and the journey is perpetual. "Setting the Sail for the Ongoing Voyage" symbolizes the commitment to continuous improvement and growth.
- Leaders adopting the Captain Mariner Mindset understand that the journey of effective management is not a one-time expedition but an ongoing voyage. They consistently revisit and reinforce the core principles of this mindset, adapting to the changing tides of the business environment.

Nurturing the Crew's Spirit:

- Nurturing the crew's spirit is akin to maintaining morale during an extended sea voyage. Leaders recognize the importance of keeping the team motivated and engaged for the long haul.
- Just as a captain uplifts the crew during extended voyages, effective leaders consistently inspire and motivate their teams. They celebrate successes, acknowledge efforts, and foster an environment that sustains high morale and commitment.

Charting the Seas of Innovation:
- Charting new courses in uncharted waters; leaders explore innovative approaches to steer their teams towards success. "Charting the Seas of Innovation" signifies the importance of embracing change and staying ahead of industry trends.
- Leaders with the Captain Mariner Mindset remain vigilant for opportunities to innovate and adapt. They encourage a culture of creativity, empowering the team to explore new ideas and technologies to stay ahead in the dynamic business landscape.

Fostering a Legacy of Leadership:
- Leaving a legacy as a respected captain; leaders focus on building a lasting legacy of effective leadership. "Fostering a Legacy of Leadership" emphasizes the enduring impact leaders can have on their teams and organizations.
- Leaders committed to the Captain Mariner Mindset understand the significance of their leadership legacy. They invest in mentoring and developing future leaders, ensuring a continuity of effective management practices that outlast their tenure.

Encouragement for the Ongoing Journey:
- Offering a captain's encouragement during challenging seas; leaders provide continual support and guidance to their teams. "Encouragement for the Ongoing Journey" is a reminder that leadership is a journey, not a destination.
- Leaders consistently offer encouragement and support to their teams. They understand that challenges are inevitable, but with a positive mindset and continuous encouragement, they can navigate through rough seas and emerge stronger.